F-4
Phantom II

AF249053

 in detail & scale

Bert Kinzey

Published
by

Aero Publishers, Inc.
U.S.A.

Arms and Armour Press
London - Melbourne

COPYRIGHT © 1981 BY DETAIL & SCALE, INC.

CONTRIBUTORS:

Ray Leader	Al Lloyd
Robert J. Mills, Jr.	Warren Munkasy
John Kunhert	Andre Wilderdijk
Roger M. Jackson	Ron Thurlow
Dana Bell	Bob Leavitt
Kent Veltman	Mike Campbell
Larry Potoski	Cliff Bossie
Tom Dunbar	Jim Chaconas
The U.S. Air Force	McDonnell Douglas

The Washington D.C. Chapter of IPMS/USA

Detail & Scale, Inc. wishes to express a special thanks to Colonel Doyle and Chief Master Sergeant Phillips of the 106th Tactical Reconnaissance Squadron, Alabama Air National Guard.

Most photographs and all drawings in this book are credited to their contributors. Photos with no credit indicated were taken by the author.

PRINTING 3 4 5 6 7 8 9

Published in United States by

Aero Publishers, Inc.
329 W. Aviation Road,
Fallbrook, CA 92028

Published in Great Britain by

Arms and Armour Press,
Lionel Leventhal Limited,
2-6 Hampstead High Street,
London NW3 1QQ,
and in Australia at
4-12
Melbourne, Victoria 3000

Library of Congress Cataloging in
Publication Data:
Kinzey, Bert
F-4 Phantom II in detail and scale
Contents: pt. 1: USAF—F-4C, F-4D, RF-4C.
1. Phantom (Fighter planes) I. Title.
UG1242.F5K526   623.74'64   81-67593 AACR2

ISBN 0-8168-5011-9 (Pt. 1) USA

British Library Cataloging in
Publication Data:
Kinzey, Bert
F-4 Phantom (USA) in detail and scale.
(Detail and scale series; 1) Part 1
1. Phantom (Fighter Planes)—History
623.74'64   UG 1242.F5

ISBN-0-85368-501-0 UK

Printed and Published in the USA by Aero Publishers, Inc.

Front Cover: F-4C-16-MC, 63-7436, of the 57th FIS at the 1976 William Tell competition.
Rear Cover: Front cockpit of an RF-4C.

F-4C-21-MC, 63-7693, of the 58th TFW at Luke AFB, October, 1976.   *(Wilderdijk)*

INTRODUCTION

Much has been written about McDonnell's "Phabulous Phatom," and one might think that there would be very little demand for another book on the F-4. But Detail & Scale has received more than twice as many requests for a book on the Phantom than for any other aircraft. In order to answer these requests, and to provide extensive coverage of the many versions of the F-4, this book is the first of three volumes that will be developed by Detail & Scale on the Phantom.

Two volumes will be dedicated to U.S. Air Force Phantoms. This book is the first of these two voumes, and covers the F-4C, F-4D, and RF-4C. A later volume will cover the F-4E and F-4G "Wild Weasel" versions as used by the U.S. Air Force. The third volume will cover the versions of the Phantom used by the U.S. Navy and Marine Corps.

The most important aspect in providing detailed coverage of an aircraft is accuracy. To insure accuracy extensive research was conducted in the preparation of this publication including coordination with McDonnell Douglas and the U.S. Air Force. For example, the 1/72nd scale five-view drawings were developed from loft-line drawings and other scale drawings provided by McDonnell Douglas. Cockpit drawings, and other detail drawings were provided by the Air Force, and come directly from flight and maintenance manuals rather than being the interpretations of civilian artists. Technical data is from the official Air Force "Standard Aircraft Characteristics" tables. Performance data is given for various missions under operational conditions, and not for speed record runs or other "optomized" conditions as usually given in other publications. With a very few exceptions, the photos in this book have never before been published. In fact, most were taken specifically for use in this publication. It has taken the efforts of many contributors over three years to compile the information, photographs, and drawings that appear on the following pages. These efforts have all been aimed at providing the best detailed coverage of the F-4C, F-4D, and RF-4C that is available in any single publication.

F-4C-24-MC, 64-0879 of the 81st TFW at Bentwaters. Note that this aircraft does not have an IR sensor which is unusual for an F-4C. Air Force Phantoms originally wore the same paint scheme as Navy Phantoms. The scheme consisted of light gull gray on upper surfaces with white underneath and on control surfaces. Also note the "buzz numbers" on the side of the fuselage. Until they were discontinued, "buzz numbers" were also carried on the underside of the fuselage between the engines. (Wilderdijk)

HISTORICAL SUMMARY

As World War II came to an end, companies that had produced military aircraft for America's war effort found themselves facing two major problems. First, the end of the war caused massive cutbacks on orders, and in many cases outright cancellation of projects resulted. Overnight, aircraft manufacturers were having to reduce their operations and lay off thousands of workers. The second problem was that aviation was at the dawn of the jet age, and the years immediately after the war would see the most radical changes in propulsion systems and airframe design in the history of the airplane. How each company was able to deal with these two problems would spell the difference between success and failure. Some well known manufacturers faded from the scene, or were absorbed by other companies. Others, relatively unknown during the war, soon developed into giants in the industry. The McDonnell Aircraft Corporation of St. Louis was one of the companies that fell into the second category.

Having served primarily as a sub-contractor during the war, McDonnell seized on the opportunity to enter the jet age since jet propulsion was already an area under exploration at St. Louis. Although the end of hostilities did cause problems and shake-ups in the aircraft industry, it also provided more time to be spent on research and development since less time was required for massive production.

McDonnell's engineers had already begun work on its first jet fighter before the war ended. Design work on the XFD-1, later to become the FH-1 Phantom, began in 1942. However, it was not until after the war that the aircraft took to the air. As the first Phantom lifted off from the USS Franklin D. Roosevelt in July 1946, McDonnell Aircraft Corporation and U.S. Naval Aviation entered the jet age in earnest.

The change from pistons to jet turbines as the means for aircraft propulsion carried many problems with it, but the use of jets in naval aviation posed even more problems. Indeed, these problems jeopardized the very existence of naval carrier-based aviation. Jets, with their high landing speeds, heavier weight, longer take-off rolls, and ability to make crispy critters out of unwary deck personnel, seemed to spell the obsolescence of the aircraft carrier which had ruled the seas in World War II.

Although powerful new catapults, new arresting gear, canted (or angled) decks, proper aircraft design to minimize approach speeds, and new handling procedures solved the problems of using jets onboard ship, these solutions took years to evolve, and admittedly, early naval jet fighters suffered from limitations imposed by considerations for shipboard operations. This was in contrast to the war years when the Navy's F4U Corsair was the equal of, if not better than, the best fighters in the Army Air Corps.

By the early 1950's, the Navy had fallen behind the U.S. Air Force in the development of jet aircraft. This was dramatized in the skies over Korea where the USAF F-86 Sabre was clearly the class of U.S. fighters. The Navy's F9F Panther proved its worth in attacking ground targets, but neither the Panther, nor McDonnell's F2H Banshee, could match the performance of the F-86 or the communist MiG-15 when it came to air-to-air combat. Therefore the Navy was obliged to seek a "navalized" version of the F-86 which subsequently developed into the FJ Fury series. This left the Navy's pride "smarting" over having to modify an Air Force aircraft for carrier use rather than being able to come up with a design of their own.

As the fifties progressed the problems of operating jets from carriers were solved, and the situation changed. The new Forrestal class of aircraft carriers were designed incorporating features that permitted them to operate the newer and "hotter" jets that were coming off of the drawing boards. Aircraft such as the F4D Skyray and F8U Crusader were developed by the Navy and were every bit the equal of their Air Force counterparts

McDonnell Aircraft Corporation had played a part in developing jet aircraft for the Navy during this period of transition. The XFD-1 mentioned earlier had become the FH-1 Phantom, and after a relatively small production run, this aircraft gave way to the F2H Banshee. These straight-wing jet fighters were followed by the swept-wing F3H Demon, but like its two predecessors, the Demon met with only moderate success.

Then on May 27, 1958, a new Navy fighter took to the air from St. Louis' Lambert Field. McDonnell Aircraft and the U.S. Navy had arrived, and the tables were turned! The F4H Phantom II was on the scene, and it began proving its superiority by establishing a long list of speed, altitude, and time-to-climb records.

As it entered service, it was now time for the Air Force to take a look at a Navy fighter. The F-4 could fly faster, higher, further, and carry more ordnance than anything in the Air Force inventory. There was no choice but to "borrow" some Navy F-4B's and test them for USAF suitability. These tests soon led

F-4C-20-MC, 63-7654, in overall gray scheme as seen at China Lake Naval Weapons Center in October 1976. This aircraft is from Edwards AFB, California, and has a long instrumentation probe on the nose. (Wilderdijk)

F-4C, F-4D, RF-4C PRODUCTION BLOCKS AND SERIAL NUMBERS
(AS ORDERED)

F-4C		
Block	**No. Built**	**Serial Numbers**
F-4C-15-MC	1	62-12199
F-4C-15-MC	14	63-7407/63-7420
F-4C-16-MC	22	63-7421/63-7442
F-4C-17-MC	26	63-7443/63-7468
F-4C-18-MC	58	63-7469/63-7526
F-4C-19-MC	71	63-7527/63-7597
F-4C-20-MC	65	63-7598/63-7662
F-4C-21-MC	51	63-7663/63-7713
F-4C-21-MC	19	64-654/64-672
F-4C-22-MC	65	64-673/64-737
F-4C-23-MC	80	64-738/64-817
F-4C-24-MC	64	64-818/64-881
F-4C-25-MC	47	64-882/64-928
F-4C-24-MC	9	64-929/64-937 *
F-4C-25-MC	26	64-938/64-963 *
F-4C-26-MC	17	64-964/64-980 *

*These last 3 blocks were ordered as F-4C, but were upgraded to F-4D standards while still in production. They are usually counted in F-4D production totals.

F-4D		
Block	**No. Built**	**Serial Numbers**
F-4D-26-MC	32	65-580/65-611
F-4D-27-MC	54	65-612/65-665
F-4D-28-MC	105	65-666/65-770
F-4D-29-MC	31	65-771/65-801
F-4D-29-MC	58	66-226/66-283
F-4D-29-MC	50	66-7455/66-7504
F-4D-30-MC	146	66-7505/66-7650
F-4D-31-MC	124	66-7651/66-7774
F-4D-31-MC	14	66-8685/66-8698
F-4D-32-MC	88	66-8699/66-8786
F-4D-33-MC	39	66-8787/8825

RF-4C		
Block	**No. Built**	**Serial Numbers**
RF-4C-16-MC	2	63-7740/63-7741
RF-4C-17-MC	1	63-7742
RF-4C-18-MC	7	63-7743/63-7749
RF-4C-19-MC	14	63-7750/63-7763
RF-4C-20-MC	21	64-997/64-1017
RF-4C-21-MC	20	64-1018/64-1037
RF-4C-22-MC	24	64-1038/64-1061
RF-4C-23-MC	16	64-1062/64-1077
RF-4C-24-MC	8	64-1078/64-1085
RF-4C-24-MC	21	64-818/64-838
RF-4C-25-MC	26	65-839/65-864
RF-4C-26-MC	37	65-865/65-901
RF-4C-27-MC	31	65-902/65-932
RF-4C-28-MC	13	65-933/65-945
RF-4C-28-MC	4	66-383/66-386
RF-4C-29-MC	1	66-387
RF-4C-28-MC	1	66-388
RF-4C-29-MC	18	66-389/66-406
RF-4C-30-PRC	22	66-407/66-428
RF-4C-31-MC	22	66-429/66-450
RF-4C-32-MC	22	66-451/66-472
RF-4C-33-MC	6	66-473/66-478
RF-4C-33-MC	15	67-428/67-442
RF-4C-34-MC	11	67-443/67-453
RF-4C-35-MC	8	67-454/67-461
RF-4C-36-MC	8	67-462/67-469
RF-4C-37-MC	14	68-548/68-561
RF-4C-38-MC	15	68-562/68-576
RF-4C-39-MC	17	68-577/68-593
RF-4C-40-MC	18	68-594/68-611
RF-4C-41-MC	9	69-349/69-357
RF-4C-42-MC	9	69-358/69-366
RF-4C-43-MC	9	69-367/69-375
RF-4C-44-MC	9	69-376/69-384
RF-4C-48-MC	5	71-248/71-252
RF-4C-49-PRC	7	71-253/71-259
RF-4C-51-MC	4	71-145/71-148
RF-4C-52-MC	4	72-149/72-152
RF-4C-53-MC	4	72-153/72-156

F-4D-27-MC, 65-615, of the 48th TFW at Lakenheath, England. Aircraft wears the standard two-tone green and brown camouflage scheme over light gray undersurfaces. Note the AIM-9 launch rails on the inboard pylon with the practice bomb dispenser underneath. (Wilderdijk)

to a decision by the Air Force to purchase the Navy's new fighter for its own squadrons.

Originally called the F-110A by the Air Force, the Phantom's designation was soon standardized as "F-4" for all services with the F-4C being the first Air Force version. But whatever designation it was given, it was also called "super" and was to become the backbone of USAF tactical fighter strength for well over a decade.

Inter-service rivalry aside, the Air Force now had a new fighter as "hot" as anything in the sky, and they set about adapting it for their own requirements. The F-4B, as used by the Navy, was primarily designed as a fleet defense interceptor, but Air Force specifications, drawn up in August 1962, called for the F-4 to perform close air support, interdiction, and counter-air operations. It was to carry all types of ordnance, including air-to-ground guided missiles.

On May 27, 1963, the first Air Force F-4C made its maiden flight and exceeded Mach 2. Already 27 F-4B's, on loan from the Navy, were being used for training, and the Air Force was anxious to start accepting its own Phantoms. In doing so, the F-4C entered operational service in the Air Force on November 20, 1963 with the 4453rd Combat Crew Training Wing at MacDill AFB, Florida. The first combat unit in the Air Force to receive the Phantom was the 12th Tactical Fighter Wing, which was also based at MacDill. Their first F-4's arrived in January 1964, and the wing was operationally ready by October of that year. Less than a year later, on July 10, 1965, two F-4C's shot down two MiG-17's, and the Air Force Phantom began compiling its impressive record in Southeast Asia. Pages of that record were to see the use of new "smart bombs", air-to-air fights with MiGs, air defense suppression missions, and much, much more.

But the Phantom also had problems ranging from cracked ribs to leaky fuel tanks. However, the biggest shortcoming was not structural, it was a design problem. The F-4 did not have an internal gun. The F-4 was developed when the guided missile was the coming thing, and some short-

F-4D-33-MC, 66-8797, of the 52nd TFW, in June, 1976. Note the "towel rack" LORAN antenna on the spine and the position of the control surfaces for landing.   *(Wilderdijk)*

Below: All Phantoms have what is known as "variable inlet geometry" to control air flow to the engine at speeds that range from being stationary on the ramp to in excess of Mach 2 in the air. This variable geometry is accomplished by two movable ramps. Bleed air vents remove excess air above and below the aft variable ramp. Air is also ducted past the fuselage fuel tanks for cooling purposes. These drawings show the workings of the air intakes, and this detail is common to all versions of the F-4.

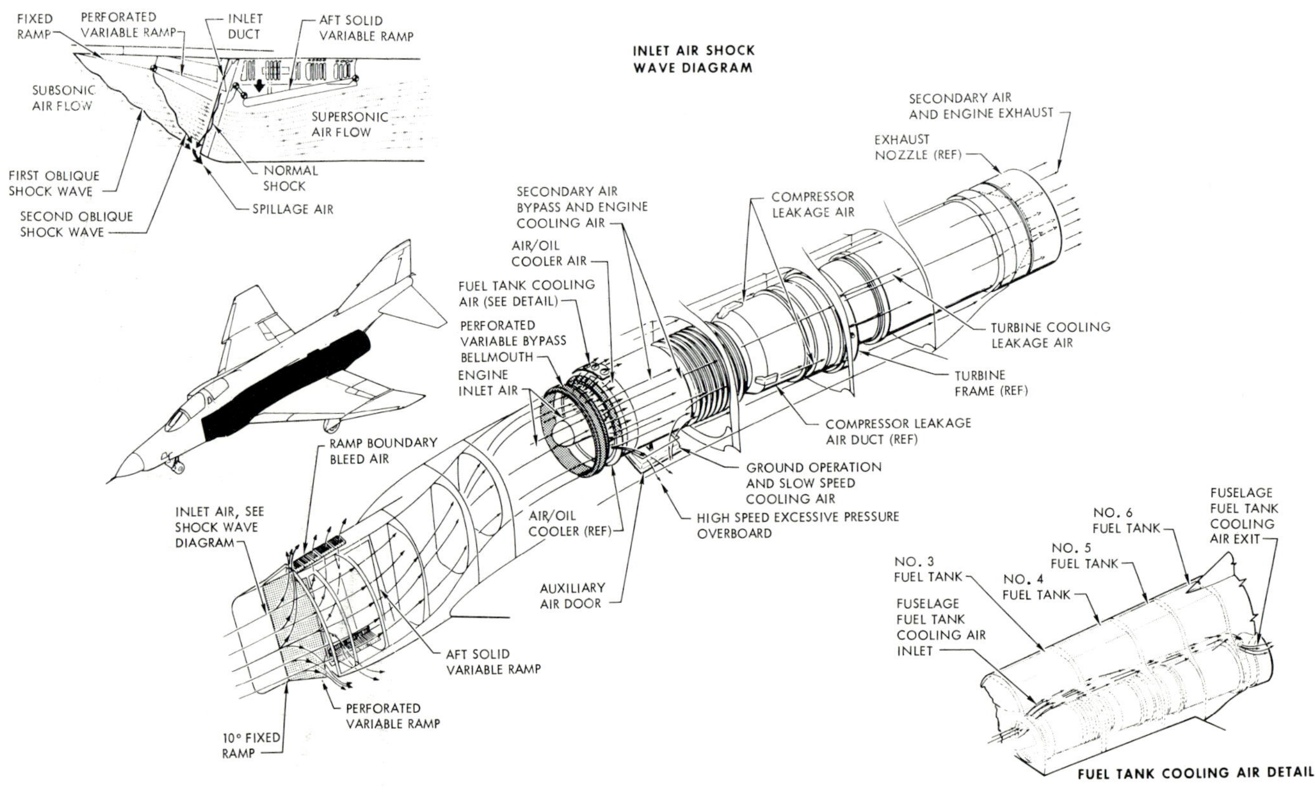

Courtesy of the U.S.A.F.

sighted planners thought that the gun was obsolete since, armed with the new missiles, no fighter would ever get in gun range of another. Therefore an internal cannon was not included in the Phantom's original design requirements. This decision can be compared to a football coach saying, "Now that we have a good passing game, we don't need any running backs." Just as the run sets up the pass in football, guns and missiles compliment each other in aerial combat. Further, the Air Force's Phantoms were to be used extensively to attack ground targets, and this made an internal gun even more necessary. The gun pods developed for the F-4 were simply not as effective as an internal gun would be. Later the Air Force would have an internal gun, but that version, the F-4E, was not available when hostilities began in Vietnam. Fortunately, the mistake of deleting the gun was a "lesson learned" with the Phantom, and all subsequent fighters, to include the latest coming off of the drawing boards and production lines, all feature an internal cannon.

The Air Force also adapted the F-4C to a reconnaissance version designated the RF-4C. In addition to its photographic missions, the RF-4C was fitted with the cabability of delivering nuclear weapons. This version entered operational service on September 24, 1964, but the first unit, the 16th TRS, was not declared combat ready until August 1965.

Following the F-4C in production was the F-4D. It possessed an improved bombing capability for hitting targets on the ground, and it had a lead computing gunsight to improve chances of hitting targets in the air, even though it still had no internal gun. This version became operational at Elgin AFB with the 33rd TFW in June of 1966.

Externally the F-4D was practically identical to the F-4C, and it required a keen eye to tell a -C from a -D simply by looking at them. A total of 793-D's were accepted by the Air Force as compared to 583 F-4C's.

The F-4E, and its derivative, the F-4G "Wild Weasel", will be covered in <u>USAF Phantoms in Detail & Scale (Part II)</u>.

RF-4C-23-MC, 64-1073, at Alconbury, England in 1966. This aircraft belongs to the 10th TRW, and wears the gull gray over white scheme. "Buzz numbers" for the Phantom consisted of the letter "F" for fighter, the letter "J," which was the letter designator for the F-4, and then the last three digits of the serial number. (Wilderdijk)

F-4C-21-MC, 63-7665, from Luke AFB, as seen at Holloman AFB, New Mexico in the summer of 1979.

F-4C DEVELOPMENT

Once the decision was made for the Air Force to buy the Phantom, the Navy issued contracts to McDonnell on behalf of the Air Force. The first contract was issued in March, 1962, and was for the aircraft only. The Air Force issued its own contract to General Electric for the J79-GE-15 engines that were to power the F-4C.

On August 29, 1962, the Air Force issued Specific Operational Requirements, SOR 200, which required the aircraft to perform close air support, interdiction, and counter-air missions. This was considerably broader in scope than the fleet defense role that was the primary mission of the Navy's Phantom.

Being the first Air Force version of the Phantom, the F-4C was closely related to the Navy's F-4B. This was due in part to the fact that Secretary of Defense Robert McNamara seemed to be obsessed with "commonality." It was during this same time period that the TFX program was being studied, and the Secretary believed that commonality could be carried to such an extent that one aircraft could be built to fill all of the needs of the Air Force and the Navy. This, of course, is the story of the F-111, and will be covered in another volume, but this policy of commonality limited the changes that the Air Force could make to the Phantom.

One of the major physical changes was the use of larger tires on the main landing gear. The Navy tires were too thin and too hard for long roll-outs on hot runways, so their width was increased from 7.7 inches to 11.5 inches. This required a bulge to be added to the top and bottom of the wing and to the landing gear doors in order to accomodate the tires when retracted. Additionally, more powerful brakes were added to the main gear.

The Air Force installed dual controls, and a rated pilot was assigned to the rear seat. The Navy's "probe and drogue" in-flight refueling system was replaced by a receptable on the spine of the fuselage to allow the aircraft to be refueled from the Air Force's KC-135 tanker aircraft. The Air Force also used the J79-GE-15 engine which featured a cartridge self-starting system so that the F-4C could be used on airfields where there were no starter units available.

Other important changes were in the electronics, radar, and avionics systems to give the F-4C a better capability of attacking ground targets. The most important of these changes were the AN/APQ-100 radar, which provided better ground mapping, an AN/AJB-7 bombing system with a sequential timer, and an AN/ASN-48 inertial navignation system.

It is also interesting to note that the Air Force added provisions for the Bullpup air-to-surface guided missile. This missile was developed by the Navy, and was used on such aircraft as the FJ-4 Fury and A-4 Skyhawk. However, Navy F-4B's were not certified to carry this missile.

The Air Force added a provision for the F-4C to carry the AIM-4D version of the Falcon air-to-air missile instead of the Navy's Sidewinder. Experience in Vietnam would later cause the Air Force to change back to the Sidewinder for its Phantoms.

Five-hundred, eighty-three F-4C's were delivered to the Air Force, and production ended in April, 1966. Thirty-six of these were later transferred to Spain, and others were converted to "Wild Weasel" air defense suppression aircraft. Most surviving F-4C's now serve in training roles at Luke AFB, and in the Air National Guard and Air Force Reserve.

F-4C TECHNICAL DATA

Development

Letter Contract	Mar 62
Mock-Up	Apr 62
First Flight & Delivery	May 63
First Operational Delivery (TAC)	Nov 63
Production Completed	May 66

The Airborne Missile Control Subsystem includes the AN/APQ-100 Radar System and the AN/APA-157 Radar Set Group. The all-altitude bomb control system (AN/AJB-7) is employed in special store deliveries. The AN/ASQ-19 integrates various communications, Navigation and Identification functions.

The AN/ASN-48 Inertial Navigation and AN/ASN-46 Navigation Computer Sets provide continuous computation of aircraft position, destination location, attitude and parameters and supplies appropriate signals to various subsystems. The AN/ASA-32 Automatic Flight Control Subsystem (AFCS) provides three axes stability augmentations, pilot relief modes, and mach and altitude hold.

POWER PLANT

Nr & Model	(2) J79-GE-15
Mfr	General Electric
Engine Spec Nr	E-2027
Type.	Axial
Length with A/B	208.45 in
Diameter (max)	38.3 in
Weight (dry)	3627 lb
Tail Pipe . . .	Variable Pos. Ejector
Augmentation	Afterburner

ELECTRONICS

Central Air Data Computer . .	A/A24G
Comm-Nav-Ident	AN/ASQ-19
AFCS	AN/ASA-32
Inertial Nav System . . .	AN/ASN-48
Navigational Computer . .	AN/ASN-46
Altimeter	AN/APN-155
Fire Control System	
Radar & Optical Sight .	AN/APQ-100
Radar Set Group . . .	AN/APA-157
AGM-12 Control System .	AN/ARW-77
All-Attitude Bombing Sys. .	AN/AJB-7
Timer, Sequential . . .	TD-709/AJB-7
RHAWS	AN/APR-25, -26

WEIGHTS

Loading	LB	L.F.
Empty	28,539 (A)	
Basic	28,890 (A)	
Design.	37,500	8.5 (6.5)
Combat	*38,606	8.2 (6.3)
Max T.O. . . .	†59,689	5.3 (4.1)
Max Land . . .	‡46,000	

(A) Actual
*   For Basic Mission
†   Limited by mission. Design T.O. wt is 58,000 lb; above normal tire wear may be expected above this weight.
‡   10 ft/sec design sinking speed.
Note: Load factors in ( ) are for supersonic maneuvers.

ENGINE RATINGS

S.L.S.	LB	RPM	MIN
Max:	*17,000	7685	†30
Mil:	10,900	7685	†30
Nor:	10,300	7385	Cont

* With afterburner operating
† Below 35,000 ft, 2 hours
  Above 35,000 ft

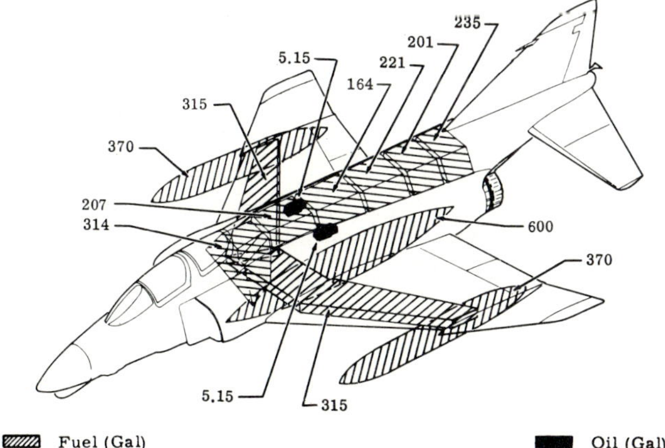

FUEL

Location	Nr Tanks	Gal
Fus, bladder	6	1342
Wgs, integral	2	630
Fus, ext, drop.	1	600
Wgs, ext, drop	2	740
	Total	3312

Grade	JP-4
Specification	MIL-J-5624

OIL

Engine, integral	2 . . .(tot) 10.3
Specification	MIL-L-7808

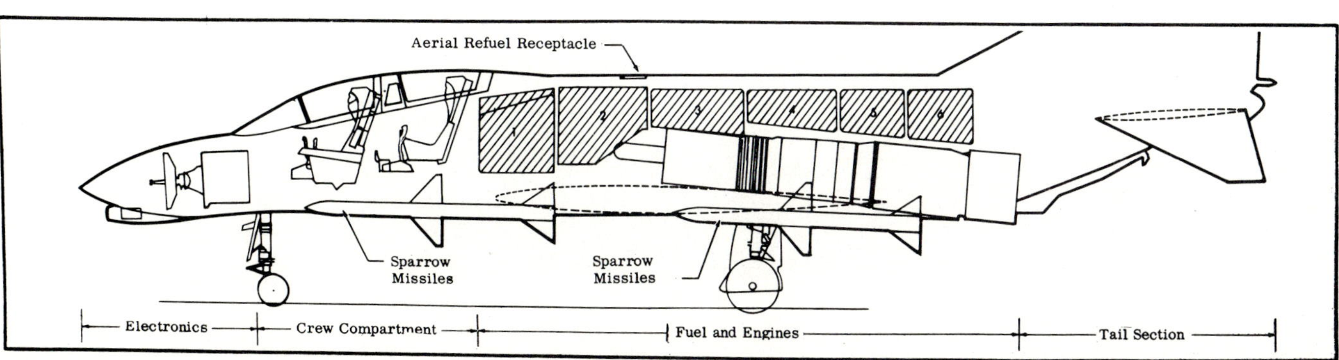

Courtesy of the U.S.A.F.

F-4C-17-MC, 63-7460, of the 57th FIS at the 1976 William Tell competition. Stripes at the top of the tail are red, white, and blue from top to bottom. Carefully note the location, size, and layout of the black and white checkerboards on the vertical tail and on top of and below the horizontal stabilizers. *(Wilderdijk)*

F-4C-24-MC, (ex USAF 64-826) as transferred to the Spanish Air Force at Torrejon, Spain. F-4's in the Spanish Air Force are designated, "C-12". *(Wilderdijk)*

F-4C-25-MC, 64-888, of the 401st TFW stationed at Torrejon, Spain approaching Ramstein AFB, Germany. *(Wilderdijk)*

F-4C-17-MC, 63-7443, making an emergency landing at Bitburg AFB, Germany. The aircraft belongs to the 52nd TFW. Note the lowered tail hook, and the ECM pod in the forward right AIM-7 bay. *(Wilderdijk)*

F-4C PERFORMANCE DATA

TYPE OF MISSION		Ground Attack Mission	Ground Attack Mission	C.A.P. Mission	Ferry Mission
EXTERNAL STORES LOADING		(4)AIM-7 + (6)M-117 + (1)600 + (2)370 Gal. Tks.	(4)AIM-7 + (11)M-117 + (2)370 Gal. Tks.	(4) AIM-7 + (1)600 + (2)370 Gal. Tks.	Clean + (1)600 + (2)370 Gal. Tks.
Take-Off Weight (lb.)		59,453	59,689	53,797	51,977
Fuel at 6.5 lb/gal (grade JP-4) (lb)		12,818/8710	12,818/4810	12,818/8710	12,818/8710
Payload - Missiles (lb)		1820	1820	1820	None
Payload - Bombs (lb)		4938	9053	None	None
Wing Loading (lb/sq ft)		112.2	112.6	101.5	98.1
Stall Speed (power off) (kn)		154.5	154.8	146.7	144.1
Take-Off Ground Run at S.L. ① (ft)		4260	4300	3380	3120
Take-Off to Clear 50 Feet ① (ft)		5200	5250	4130	3820
Rate of Climb at S.L. ② (fpm)		5900	5260	8210	8900
Rate of Climb at S.L. (One Engine Out) ① (fpm)		4810	4180	7470	8200
Time: S.L. to 20,000 ft. ②⑦ (min)		5.61	6.95	3.60	3.18
Time: S.L. to 30,000 ft. ②⑦ (min)		12.85 ④	12.70 ⑤	7.05	6.30
Service Ceiling (100 FPM) ② (ft)		26,800	24,350	33,050	34,400
Service Ceiling (One Engine Out) ① (ft)		25,500	22,450	32,900	34,250
Combat Range ③ (n mi)		———	———	———	1528
Combat Radius ③ (n mi)		468	284	250	———
Average Cruise Speed (kn)		492	478	502	501
Initial Cruising Altitude (ft)		25,950	24,450	30,400	31,250
Final Cruising Altitude (ft)		38,000	37,700	39,700	39,700
Total Mission Time (hr)		2.18	1.47	2.48/1.39 ⑥	3.05
Combat Weight (lb)		40,591	38,915	36,140	32,192
Combat Altitude (ft)		S.L.	S.L.	40,000	39,700
Combat Speed ①②⑧ (kn)		741/622	718/612	1178/——	1205/546
Combat Climb ①② (fpm)		41,000/11,800	40,650/11,610	13,100/1230	11,400/2480
Max Speed at 40,000 ft. ① (kn)		1112	1048	1188	1210
Basic Speed at 35,000 ft. ①⑧ (kn)		1106	1046	1183	1204
Landing Weight (lb)		34,878	35,002	32,192	32,192
Ground Roll at S.L. (ft)		3205	3215	2975	2975
Ground Roll (Parabrake) (ft)		2505	2510	2320	2320
Total from 50 ft. (ft)		4290	4300	4000	4000
Total from 50 ft. (Parabrake) (ft.)		3600	3605	3350	3350

NOTES: ① Maximum Power   ② Military Power   ③ Detailed Description of Missions are given below.   ④ Time to Mil. Powr. Combat Ceiling (27,500 ft.)   ⑤ Time to Mil. Powr. Combat Ceiling (25,150 ft.)   ⑥ Mission Time/C.A.P. Time   ⑦ Allows for weight reduction during ground operation and climb   ⑧ Installed engine flight limits at SL and 35,000 ft. are 760 and 1170 kts, respectively.

DESCRIPTION OF GROUND ATTACK MISSIONS

Take-off with maximum thrust, climb on course with military thrust to optimum cruise altitude, cruise out at long range speeds, descend to sea level (no credit for fuel or distance), search out target for five minutes at military thrust, expend stores, climb on course with military thrust to optimum cruise altitude, cruise back at long range speeds. Range free allowances include 5 minutes at normal thrust and 1 minute at max thrust at sea level static for starting engines and take-off, 5 minutes search at sea level at military thrust; and a reserve of 20 minutes loiter at sea level at speeds for maximum endurance (two engines) plus 5% of initial fuel load.

DESCRIPTION OF COMBAT AIR PATROL (CAP) MISSION

Take-off with maximum thrust, climb on course with military thrust to optimum cruise altitude, cruise out at long range speeds (climb and cruise = 250 n. miles), patrol at max endurance altitude, climb at maximum thrust to acceleration altitude (40,000 ft.), accelerate at maximum thrust to Mach = 1.5 at 40,000 ft. and remain at this speed and altitude for 2 minutes, expend missiles, cruise back at long range speed. Range free allowances include 5 minutes at normal thrust and 1 minute at maximum thrust at sea level for starting engines and take-off; and a reserve of 20 minutes loiter at sea level for starting engines and take-off; and a reserve of 20 minutes loiter at sea level at speeds for maximum endurance (two engines) plus 5% of initial fuel load.

DESCRIPTION OF FERRY MISSION

Take-off with maximum thrust, climb on course with military thrust to optimum cruise altitude, cruise out at long range speeds to remote base. Range free allowances include 5 minutes at normal thrust and 1 minute at maximum thrust at sea level static for starting engines and take-off; and a reserve of 20 minutes loiter at sea level at speeds for maximum endurance (two engines) plus 5% of initial fuel load.

Data and information courtesy of the U.S. Air Force.

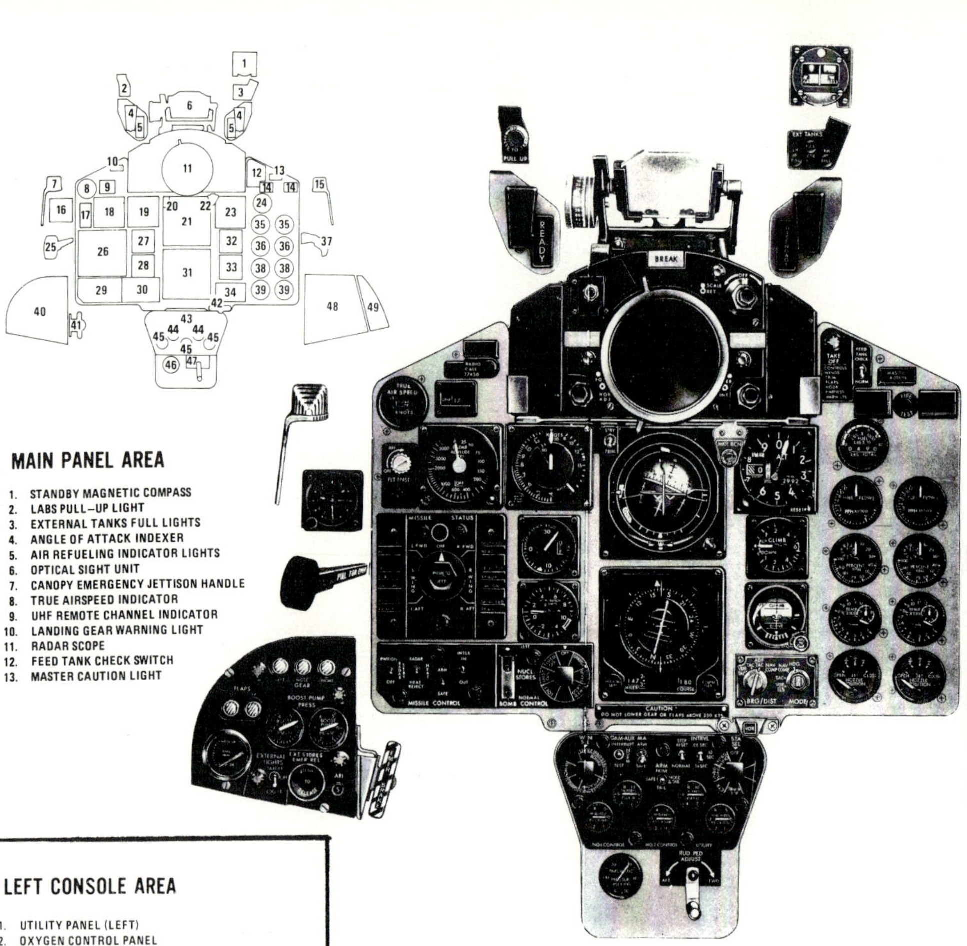

FRONT COCKPIT
TYPICAL F-4C
Courtesy of the U.S.A.F.

14. FIRE—OVERHEAT WARNING LIGHTS
15. CANOPY MANUAL UNLOCK HANDLE
16. EIGHT DAY CLOCK
17. FLIGHT INSTRUMENT LIGHTS
   CONTROL PANEL
18. RADAR ALTIMETER
19. AIRSPEED AND MACH INDICATOR
20. REFERENCE SYSTEM SELECTOR SWITCH
21. ALTITUDE DIRECTOR INDICATOR (ADI)
22. MARKER BEACON LIGHT
23. ALTIMETER
24. INTERNAL FUEL QUANTITY INDICATOR
25. LANDING GEAR CONTROL HANDLE

26. MISSILE STATUS PANEL
27. ANGLE OF ATTACK INDICATOR
28. ACCELEROMETER
29. MISSILE CONTROL PANEL
30. BOMB CONTROL PANEL
31. HORIZONTAL SITUATION INDICATOR (HSI)
32. VERTICAL VELOCITY INDICATOR
33. EMERGENCY ATTITUDE INDICATOR
34. NAVIGATION FUNCTION SELECTOR PANEL
35. FUEL FLOW INDICATORS
36. TACHOMETERS
37. ARRESTING HOOK CONTROL HANDLE
38. EXHAUST GAS TEMPERATURE INDICATORS

MAIN PANEL AREA

1. STANDBY MAGNETIC COMPASS
2. LABS PULL—UP LIGHT
3. EXTERNAL TANKS FULL LIGHTS
4. ANGLE OF ATTACK INDEXER
5. AIR REFUELING INDICATOR LIGHTS
6. OPTICAL SIGHT UNIT
7. CANOPY EMERGENCY JETTISON HANDLE
8. TRUE AIRSPEED INDICATOR
9. UHF REMOTE CHANNEL INDICATOR
10. LANDING GEAR WARNING LIGHT
11. RADAR SCOPE
12. FEED TANK CHECK SWITCH
13. MASTER CAUTION LIGHT

39. EXHAUST NOZZLE POSITION INDICATORS
40. LEFT SUB—PANEL
41. EMERGENCY BRAKE CONTROL HANDLE
42. VOR MODE LIGHT
43. MULTIPLE WEAPONS CONTROL PANEL
44. OIL PRESSURE INDICATORS
45. HYDRAULIC PRESSURE INDICATORS
46. PNEUMATIC PRESSURE INDICATORS
47. RUDDER PEDAL ADJUSTMENT CRANK
48. RIGHT SUB—PANEL (TELELIGHTS)
49. INSTRUMENT LIGHTS INTENSITY
   CIRCUIT BREAKERS

LEFT CONSOLE AREA

1. UTILITY PANEL (LEFT)
2. OXYGEN CONTROL PANEL
3. AGM—12 CONTROL HANDLE
4. ENGINE CONTROL PANEL (INBOARD)
5. DRAG CHUTE CONTROL HANDLE
6. VOR/ILS CONTROL PANEL
7. AUTOMATIC FLIGHT CONTROL SYSTEM
   CONTROL PANEL
8. BOARDING STEPS POSITION INDICATOR
9. INTERCOM SYSTEM CONTROL PANEL
10. BLANK PANEL
11. BLANK PANEL
12. ARMAMENT SAFETY OVERRIDE SWITCH
13. ANTI-G SUIT CONTROL VALVE
14. OUTBOARD PYLON JETTISON SELECT
   SWITCH
15. AUXILIARY ARMAMENT CONTROL PANEL
16. FUEL CONTROL PANEL
17. RAM AIR TURBINE CONTROL HANDLE
18. EXTRA PICTURE SWITCH
19. CANOPY SELECTOR
20. FLAP CONTROL PANEL
21. EJECT LIGHT/SWITCH
22. ENGINE CONTROL PANEL (OUTBOARD)
23. THROTTLES

RIGHT CONSOLE AREA

1. CNI EQUIPMENT COOLING RESET BUTTON
2. EMERGENCY VENT HANDLE
3. UTILITY PANEL (RIGHT)
4. DEFOG/FOOT HEAT CONTROL PANEL
5. CIRCUIT BREAKER PANEL
6. TEMPERATURE CONTROL PANEL
7. EMERGENCY FLOODLIGHTS PANEL
8. COCKPIT LIGHTS CONTROL PANEL
9. STANDBY ATTITUDE CIRCUIT BREAKER AND
   INTENSITY CONTROL PANEL
10. INSTRUMENT LIGHTS INTENSITY
   CONTROL PANEL
11. EXTERIOR LIGHTS CONTROL PANEL
12. UTILITY ELECTRICAL RECEPTACLE
13. BLANK PANEL
14. COMPASS CONTROL PANEL
15. CLUSTER BOMB UNIT CONTROL PANEL
16. DCU—94A BOMB CONTROL—MONITOR PANEL
17. IFF CONTROL PANEL
18. NAVIGATION CONTROL PANEL
19. COMMUNICATION CONTROL PANEL
20. GENERATOR CONTROL PANEL

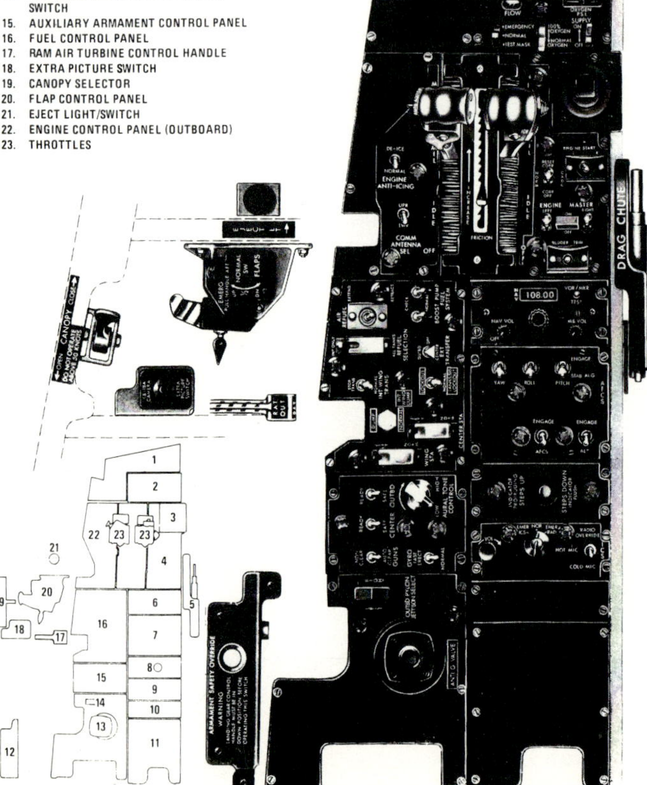
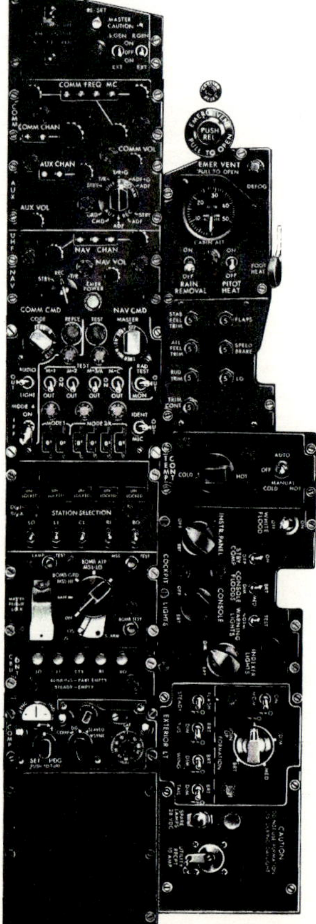

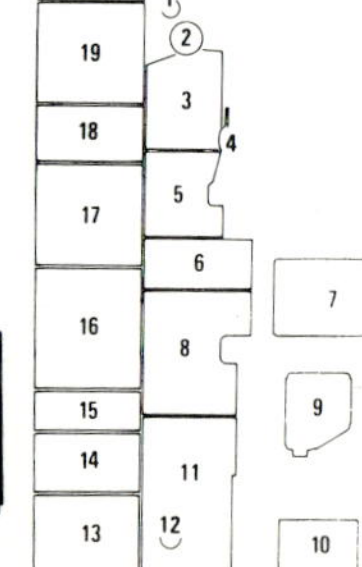

MAIN PANEL AREA

Courtesy of the U.S.A.F.

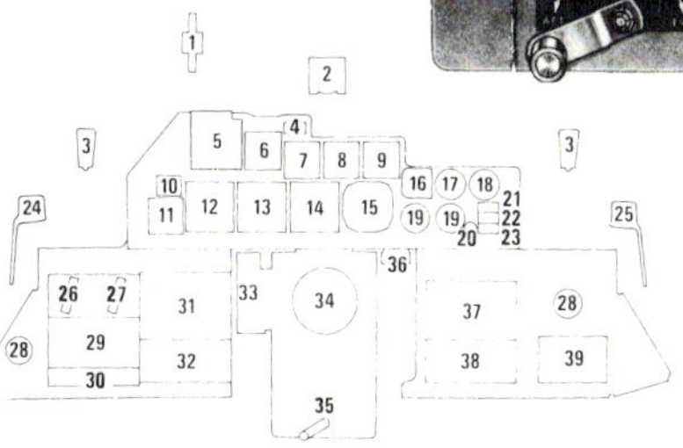

1. COMMAND SELECTOR VALVE
2. STANDBY MAGNETIC COMPASS
3. ANGLE OF ATTACK INDEXER
4. MASTER CAUTION LIGHT
5. COURSE INDICATOR
6. ANGLE OF ATTACK INDICATOR
7. EIGHT DAY CLOCK
8. ACCELEROMETER
9. TURN AND SLIP INDICATOR
10. UHF CHANNEL REMOTE INDICATOR
11. VERTICAL VELOCITY INDICATOR
12. ALTIMETER
13. ATTITUDE INDICATOR
14. AIRSPEED–MACH INDICATOR
15. BEARING–DISTANCE–HEADING INDICATOR
16. NAVIGATION FUNCTION SELECTOR PANEL
17. GROUND SPEED INDICATOR
18. TRUE AIRSPEED INDICATOR
19. TACHOMETERS
20. RADAR–CNI COOLING RESET BUTTON
21. CANOPY UNLOCKED WARNING LIGHT
22. INERTIAL NAVIGATOR OUT WARNING LIGHT
23. RADAR–CNI COOL OFF WARNING LIGHT
24. CANOPY EMERGENCY JETTISON HANDLE
25. CANOPY MANUAL UNLOCK HANDLE
26. EMERGENCY LANDING GEAR CONTROL HANDLE
27. EMERGENCY BRAKE CONTROL HANDLE
28. AIR VENT NOZZLES
29. OXYGEN CONTROL PANEL
30. BLANK PANEL
31. BLANK PANEL
32. LANDING GEAR–FLAP INDICATOR PANEL
33. DIRECT READING SCOPE CAMERA
34. RADAR SCOPE
35. RUDDER PEDAL ADJUSTMENT CRANK
36. EJECT LIGHT
37. BLANK PANEL
38. LABS RELEASE ANGLE CONTROL PANEL
39. BOMBING TIMER CONTROL PANEL

LEFT CONSOLE AREA

1. AUXILIARY RADAR CONTROL PANEL
2. RADAR CONTROL PANEL
3. COMMUNICATION CONTROL PANEL
4. NAVIGATION CONTROL PANEL
5. INTERCOM CONTROL PANEL
6. BLANK PANEL
7. STALL WARNING TONE CONTROL PANEL
8. MARKER BEACON VOR/ILS AUDIO CONTROL PANEL
9. ANTI–G SUIT CONTROL VALVE
10. OXYGEN QUANTITY GAGE
11. CABIN ALTIMETER
12. BLANK PANEL
13. PULL UP TONE CUTOUT SWITCH
14. EMERGENCY FLAP CONTROL PANEL
15. CANOPY SELECTOR
16. THROTTLES
17. BLANK PANEL
18. CIRCUIT BREAKER PANEL NO. 5

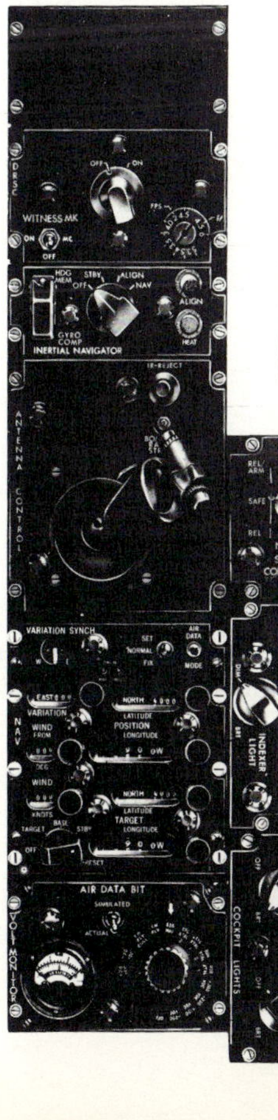

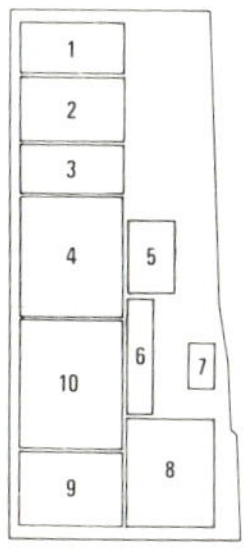

RIGHT CONSOLE AREA

1. BLANK PANEL
2. DIRECT RADAR SCOPE CAMERA CONTROL PANEL
3. INERTIAL NAVIGATOR CONTROL PANEL
4. RADAR ANTENNA CONTROL HANDLE
5. NUCLEAR CONSENT SWITCH
6. INDEXER LIGHTS CONTROL PANEL
7. SST–181X PULSE SELECTOR SWITCH
8. COCKPIT LIGHTS CONTROL PANEL
9. VOLTAGE MONITOR PANEL
10. NAVIGATION CONTROL PANEL

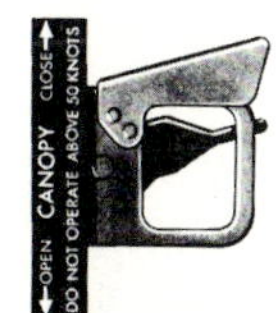
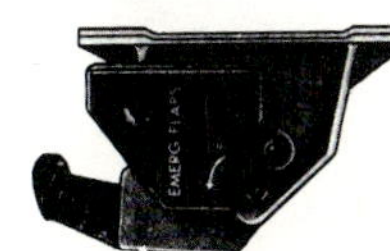
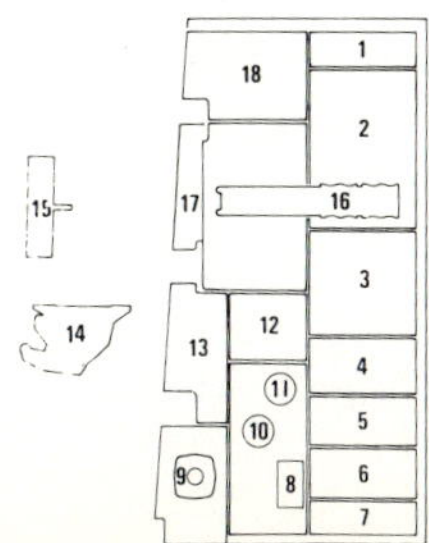
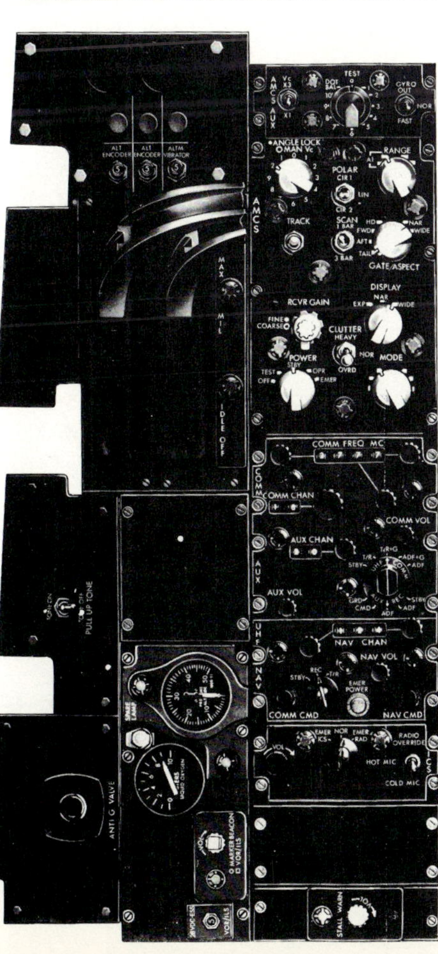

F-4D-31-MC, 66-7678, of the 334th TFS, 4th TFW, from Seymour Johnson AFB, landing at Yakota AFB, Japan, May, 1970.

(Matsuzaki via Wilderdijk)

F-4D DEVELOPMENT

Following the F-4C into production for the Air Force was the F-4D. Although practically identical to the F-4C in external appearance, the F-4D incorporated several new features that permitted the Air Force to tailor the aircraft to better meet its needs for a tactical fighter. Both air-to-air and air-to-surface capabilities were improved.

Like the F-4C, the F-4D was procured for the Air Force by the Navy. Contractual arrangements were made with McDonnell in March 1964 only two months after the first F-4C's had been received by an operational unit. The prototype first flew in June, 1965 and the first production aircraft made its first flight on December 8th of that year. By June 21, 1966 the F-4D was assigned to its first combat unit, the 33rd Tactical Fighter Wing at Eglin AFB.

The AN/APQ-109A radar was used in the F-4D. It was smaller and lighter than the radar in the F-4C and provided an air-to-ground ranging capability. An all-altitude bombing system designated AN/AJB-7 was added to be used for the delivery of nuclear weapons.

The AN/ASG-22 Lead Computing Gunsight was added to the F-4D giving the aircraft better air-to-air dog fighting capabilities. The gyro and amplifier for this sight were located behind the rear cockpit, and required that the Number 1 fuel cell be reduced in size. This resulted in a reduction of 83 gallons of internal fuel. Sharing this space with the gyro and amplifier were the AN/ASQ-91 Weapons Release Computer and the AN/ASN-63 Inertial Navigation System.

Some F-4D's were built without the IR sensor under the radome, but these were soon added. The fairing for the sensor was different from the one used on the F-4C, having a bulge on the rear half. This different sensor is about the only way to visually distinguish an F-4C from an F-4D.

From the onset, the F-4D was designed to carry the AIM-4D Falcon missile. Four could be carried on the two inboard pylons, but in a different configuration than used for the Sidewinders. Instead of one missile being carried on each side of the pylon, as was the case with the Sidewinder, one Falcon was carried beneath the pylon and the other on the inboard side of the pylon. This arrangement meant that no additional ordnance could be carried under the pylon. With Sidewinders installed in the "opposed" arrangement, other ordnance could still be carried under the pylon.

During the war in Southeast Asia, Radar Homing and Warning Systems (RHAWS) became important as a means for detecting enemy radars. The F-4D was fitted with the AN/APS-107A system. It also had the capability to deliver laser and electro-optically guided bombs and the Maverick E.O. guided missile. Additionally the F-4D was used as a "chaff bomber" laying corridors of chaff to protect other strike aircraft.

A total of 793 F-4D's were accepted by the Air Force, of which 18 were transferred to the Republic of Korea Air Force. An additional 32 F-4D's were also accepted by the Air Force for the Foreign Military Sales (FMS) program, and these were sold to Iran. Production ended in February 1968.

F-4D TECHNICAL DATA

Development

The F-4D is similar to the F-4C except air-to-air ranging and bombing capabilities have been improved. The number 1 fuel cell has been redesigned.

Letter Contract	Mar 64
First Prototype	Jun 65
First Operational Delivery	Apr 66
Production Completed	Feb 68

The Airborne Missile Control Subsystem includes the AN/APQ-109A Radar System and the AN/APA-165 or -157 Radar Set Group. The all attitude bomb control system (AN/AJB-7) is employed in special store deliveries.

The AN/ASN Inertial Navigation and AN/ASN-46A Navigation Computer Sets provide continuous computation of aircraft position, destination location, attitude and ground speed. A Central Air Data Computer (CADC) which senses aircraft air data parameters and supplies appropriate signals to various subsystems. The AN/ASA-32H Flight Control Subsystem (AFCS) provides three axis stability augmentation, pilot relief modes and mach and altitude hold.

POWER PLANT

Nr & Model	(2) J79-GE-15
Mfr	General Electric
Engine Spec Nr	E-2027
Type	Axial
Length with A/B	208.45 in
Diameter (max)	38.3 in
Weight (dry)	3627 lb
Tail Pipe	Variable Pos. Ejector
Augmentation	Afterburner

ELECTRONICS

Central Air Data Computer	A/A24G
Comm-Nav-Ident	AN/ASQ-19
AFCS	AN/ASA-32
Inertial Nav System	AN/ASN-63
Navigational Computer	AN/ASN-46A
Altimeter	AN/APN-155
Fire Control System	
Radar Set	AN/APQ-109A
Radar Set Group	AN/APA-165
Computing Sight	AN/ASG-22
AGM-12 Control System	AN/ARW-77
All-Altitude Bomb Sys	AN/AJB-7
Timer, Sequential	TD-709/AJB-7
Weapons Rel. Sys	AN/ASQ-91
RHAWS	AN/APS-107A

WEIGHTS

Loading	Lb	L.F.
Empty	28,873 (A)	
Basic	29,224	
Design	37,500	8.5 (6.5)
Combat	* 38,706	8.1 (6.2)
Max T.O.	† 59,483	5.3 (4.1)
Max Land	‡ 46,000	

(A) Actual
* For Basic Mission
† Limited by mission. Design T.O. wt is 58,000 lb; above normal tire wear may be expected above this weight.
‡ 10 ft/sec design sinking speed.
Note: Load factors in ( ) are for supersonic maneuvers.

ENGINE RATINGS

S.L.S.	LB	RPM	MIN
Max:	*17,000	7685	†30
Mil:	10,900	7685	†30
Nor:	10,300	7385	Cont

* With afterburner operating
† Below 35,000 ft, 2 hours
  Above 35,000 ft

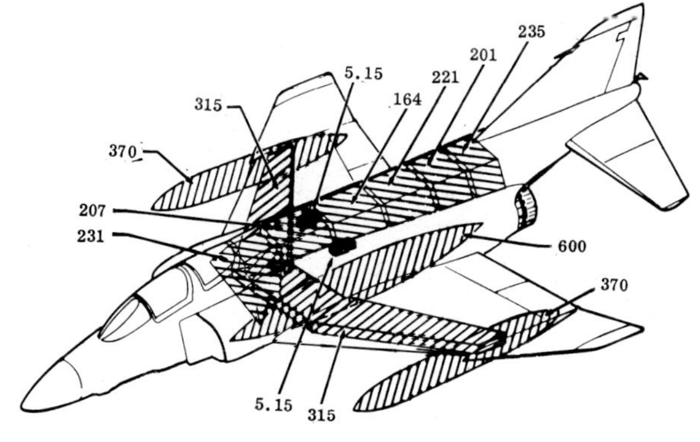

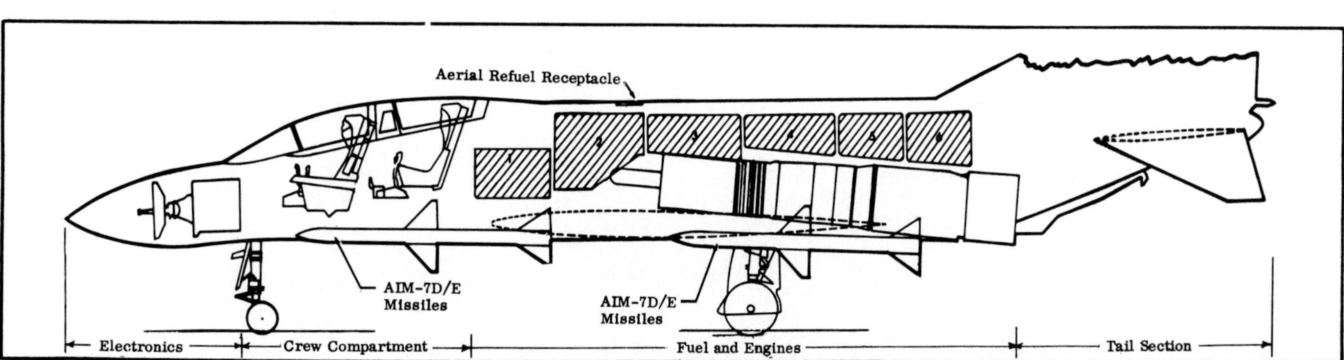

FUEL

Location	Nr Tanks	Gal
Fus, bladder	6	1259
Wgs, integral	2	630
Fus, ext, drop	1	600
Wgs, ext, drop	2	740
	Total	3229

Grade	JP-4
Specification	MIL-J-5624

OIL

Engine, integral	2 (tot) 10.3
Specification	MIL-L-7808

▨ Fuel (Gal)   ■ Oil (Gal)

Courtesy of the U.S.A.F.

F-4D-29-MC, 66-7463, with six MiG-21 kills indicated on the splitter plate. This aircraft was flown by Steve Ritchie on his first and fifth MiG kills.   *(Thurlow)*

F-4D-31-MC, 66-727, of the 52nd TFW.   *(France)*

F-4D-29-MC, 66-491, from the 335th TFS, 4th TFW in February, 1970.   *(Matsuzaki via Wilkerdijk)*

F-4D-29-MC, 66-7461, landing at Yakota AFB, Japan.   *(Matsuzaki via Wilderdijk)*

F-4D PERFORMANCE DATA

TYPE OF MISSION		Ground Attack Mission	Ground Attack Mission	C.A.P. Mission	Ferry Mission
EXTERNAL STORES LOADING		(4)AIM-7 + (6)M-117 + (1)600 + (2)370 Gal. Tks.	(4)AIM-7 + (11)M-117 + (2)370 Gal. Tks.	(4) AIM-7 + (1)600 + (2)370 Gal. Tks.	Clean + (1)600 + (2)370 Gal. Tks.
Take-Off Gross Weight	(lb.)	59,247	59,483	53,591	51,771
Fuel (JP-4, 6.5 lb/gal) (Int/Ext)	(lb)	12,278/8710	12,278/4810	12,278/8710	12,278/8710
Payload - Missiles	(lb)	1820	1820	1820	None
Payload - Bombs	(lb)	4938	9053	None	None
Wing Loading	(lb/sq ft)	111.8	112.2	101.1	97.7
Stall Speed (Appr. Pwr. BLC On, Wing Rock)	(kn)	154.1	154.5	146.4	143.9
Take-Off Ground Run at S.L. ①	(ft)	4220	4270	3360	3090
Take-Off to Clear 50 Feet ①	(ft)	5160	5200	4100	3800
Rate of Climb at S.L. ②	(fpm)	5920	5280	8240	8940
Rate of Climb at S.L. (One Engine Out) ①	(fpm)	4830	4200	7500	8250
Time: S.L. to 20,000 ft. ②⑦	(min)	5.60	6.94	3.59	3.17
Time: S.L. to 30,000 ft. ②⑦	(min)	12.85 ④	12.70 ⑤	7.03	6.28
Service Ceiling (100 FPM) ②	(ft)	26,910	24,450	33,150	34,510
Service Ceiling (One Engine Out) ①	(ft)	25,640	22,560	33,040	34,400
Combat Range ③	(n mi)	———	———	———	1469
Combat Radius ③	(n mi)	447	266	250	———
Average Speed	(kn)	492	478	503	502
Initial Cruising Altitude	(ft)	26,050	24,550	30,550	31,350
Final Cruising Altitude	(ft)	37,800	37,500	39,500	39,500
Total Mission Time	(hr)	2.09	1.40	2.36/1.27 ⑥	2.93
Combat Weight	(lb)	40,718	39,059	36,478	32,509
Combat Altitude	(ft)	S.L.	S.L.	40,000	39,500
Combat Speed ①②⑨	(kn)	741/622	718/612	1178/——	1207/547
Combat Climb ①②	(fpm)	40,900/11,780	40,600/11,570	13,000/1210	11,350/2430
Max Speed at 40,000 ft. ①	(kn)	1112	1048	1188	1210
Basic Speed at 35,000 ft. ①⑨	(kn)	1106	1046	1183	1204
Landing Weight	(lb)	35,195	35,320	32,509	32,509
Ground Roll at S.L.	(ft)	3240	3250	3000	3000
Ground Roll (Parabrake)	(ft)	2530	2540	2350	2350
Total from 50 ft.	(ft)	4320	4340	4030	4030
Total from 50 ft. (Parabrake)	(ft.)	3630	3640	3380	3380

NOTES: ① Maximum Power ② Military Power ③ Detailed Description of Missions are given below. ④ Time to Mil. Powr. Combat Ceiling (27,600 ft.) ⑤ Time to Mil. Powr. Combat Ceiling (25,200 ft.) ⑥ Mission Time/C.A.P. Time ⑦ Allows for weight reduction during ground operation and climb ⑧ Subsonic Ceiling ⑨ Installed engine flight limits at SL and 35,000 ft. are 760 and 1170 kts, respectively.

DESCRIPTION OF GROUND ATTACK MISSIONS

Take-off with maximum thrust, climb on course with military thrust to optimum cruise altitude, cruise out at long range speeds, descend to sea level (no credit for fuel or distance), search out target for five minutes at military thrust, expend stores, climb on course with military thrust to optimum cruise altitude, cruise back at long range speeds. Range free allowances include 5 minutes at normal thrust and 1 minute at max thrust at sea level static for starting engines and take-off, 5 minutes search at sea level at military thrust; and a reserve of 20 minutes loiter at sea level at speeds for maximum endurance (two engines) plus 5% of initial fuel load.

DESCRIPTION OF COMBAT AIR PATROL (CAP) MISSION

Take-off with maximum thrust, climb on course with military thrust to optimum cruise altitude, cruise out at long range speeds (climb and cruise = 250 n. miles), patrol at max endurance altitude, climb at maximum thrust to acceleration altitude (40,000 ft.), accelerate at maximum thrust to Mach = 1.5 at 40,000 ft. and remain at this speed and altitude for 2 minutes, expend missiles, cruise back at long range speed. Range free allowances include 5 minutes at normal thrust and 1 minute at maximum thrust at sea level for starting engines and take-off; and a reserve of 20 minutes loiter at sea level for starting engines and take-off; and a reserve of 20 minutes loiter at sea level at speeds for maximum endurance (two engines) plus 5% of initial fuel load.

DESCRIPTION OF FERRY MISSION

Take-off with maximum thrust, climb on course with military thrust to optimum cruise altitude, cruise out at long range speeds to remote base. Range free allowances include 5 minutes at normal thrust and 1 minute at maximum thrust at sea level static for starting engines and take-off; and a reserve of 20 minutes loiter at sea level at speeds for maximum endurance (two engines) plus 5% of initial fuel load.

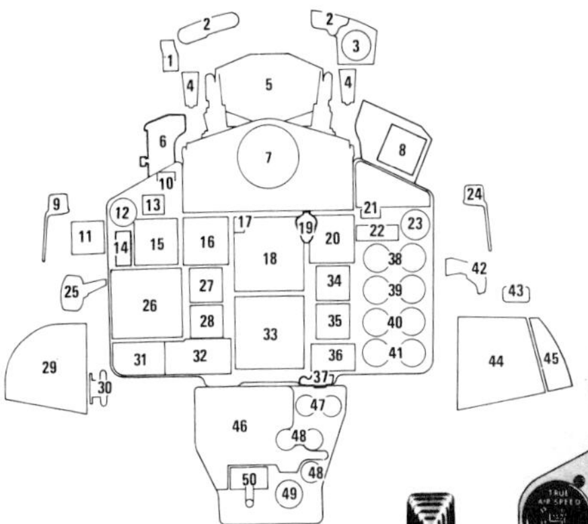

MAIN PANEL AREA

1. LABS PULL–UP LIGHT
2. AIR REFUELING INDICATOR LIGHTS
3. STANDBY MAGNETIC COMPASS
4. ANGLE OF ATTACK INDEXER
5. OPTICAL SIGHT UNIT
6. RANGE INDICATOR
7. RADAR SCOPE
8. AZIMUTH–ELEVATION INDICATOR
9. CANOPY EMERGENCY JETTISON HANDLE
10. LANDING GEAR WARNING LIGHT
11. EIGHT DAY CLOCK
12. TRUE AIRSPEED INDICATOR
13. UHF REMOTE CHANNEL INDICATOR
14. FLIGHT INSTRUMENT LIGHTS CONTROL PANEL
15. RADAR ALTIMETER
16. AIRSPEED AND MACH INDICATOR
17. REFERENCE SYSTEM SELECTOR SWITCH
18. ATTITUDE DIRECTOR INDICATOR (ADI)
19. MARKER BEACON LIGHT
20. ALTIMETER
21. MASTER CAUTION LIGHT
22. FIRE–OVERHEAT WARNING LIGHTS
23. INTERNAL FUEL QUANTITY INDICATOR
24. CANOPY MANUAL UNLOCK HANDLE
25. LANDING GEAR CONTROL HANDLE
26. MISSILE STATUS PANEL

27. ANGLE OF ATTACK INDICATOR
28. ACCELEROMETER
29. LEFT SUB–PANEL
30. EMERGENCY BRAKE CONTROL HANDLE
31. MISSILE CONTROL PANEL
32. DELIVERY MODE SELECTOR PANEL
33. HORIZONTAL SITUATION INDICATOR (HSI)
34. VERTICAL VELOCITY INDICATOR
35. EMERGENCY ATTITUDE INDICATOR
36. NAVIGATION FUNCTION SELECTOR PANEL
37. VOR MODE LIGHT
38. FUEL FLOW INDICATORS
39. TACHOMETERS
40. EXHAUST GAS TEMPERATURE INDICATORS
41. EXHAUST NOZZLE POSITION INDICATORS
42. ARRESTING HOOK CONTROL HANDLE
43. FEED TANK CHECK SWITCH
44. RIGHT SUB–PANEL (TELELIGHTS)
45. INSTRUMENT LIGHTS INTENSITY CIRCUIT BREAKERS
46. STATION AND WEAPON CONTROL PANEL
47. OIL PRESSURE INDICATORS
48. HYDRAULIC PRESSURE INDICATORS
49. PNEUMATIC PRESSURE INDICATOR
50. RUDDER PEDAL ADJUSTMENT CRANK

LEFT CONSOLE AREA

1. UTILITY PANEL (LEFT)
2. OXYGEN CONTROL PANEL
3. AGM–12B (GAM–83) CONTROL HANDLE
4. ENGINE CONTROL PANEL (INBOARD)
5. DRAG CHUTE CONTROL HANDLE
6. VOR/ILS CONTROL PANEL
7. AUTOMATIC FLIGHT CONTROL SYSTEM CONTROL PANEL
8. BOARDING STEPS POSITION INDICATOR
9. INTERCOM SYSTEM CONTROL PANEL
10. BLANK PANEL
11. BLANK PANEL
12. ARMAMENT SAFETY OVERRIDE SWITCH
13. ANTI–G SUIT CONTROL VALVE
14. OUTBOARD PYLON JETTISON SELECT SWITCH
15. ECM POD JETTISON SWITCH
16. AN/ALE–40 PROGRMMER
17. AUXILIARY ARMAMENT CONTROL PANEL
18. FUEL CONTROL PANEL
19. RAM AIR TURBINE CONTROL HANDLE
20. EXTRA PICTURE SWITCH
21. CANOPY SELECTOR
22. FLAP CONTROL PANEL
23. EJECT LIGHT/SWITCH
24. ENGINE CONTROL PANEL (OUTBOARD)
25. THROTTLES

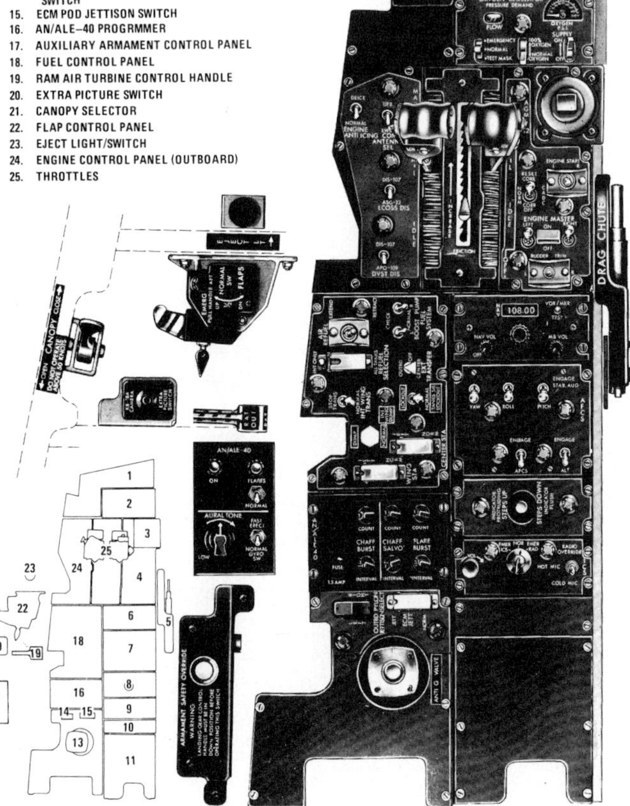

RIGHT CONSOLE AREA

1. CNI EQUIPMENT COOLING RESET BUTTON
2. EMERGENCY VENT HANDLE
3. UTILITY PANEL (RIGHT)
4. DEFOG/FOOT HEAT CONTROL HANDLE
5. CIRCUIT BREAKER PANEL
6. TEMPERATURE CONTROL PANEL
7. EMERGENCY FLOODLIGHTS PANEL
8. COCKPIT LIGHTS CONTROL PANEL
9. STANDBY ATTITUDE CIRCUIT BREAKER AND INTENSITY CONTROL PANEL
10. INSTRUMENT LIGHTS INTENSITY CONTROL PANEL
11. EXTERIOR LIGHTS CONTROL PANEL
12. UTILITY ELECTRICAL RECEPTACLE
13. BLANK PANEL
14. BLANK PANEL
15. COMPASS CONTROL PANEL
16. DCU–94A BOMB CONTROL–MONITOR PANEL
17. IFF CONTROL PANEL
18. NAVIGATION CONTROL PANEL
19. COMMUNICATION CONTROL PANEL
20. GENERATOR CONTROL PANEL

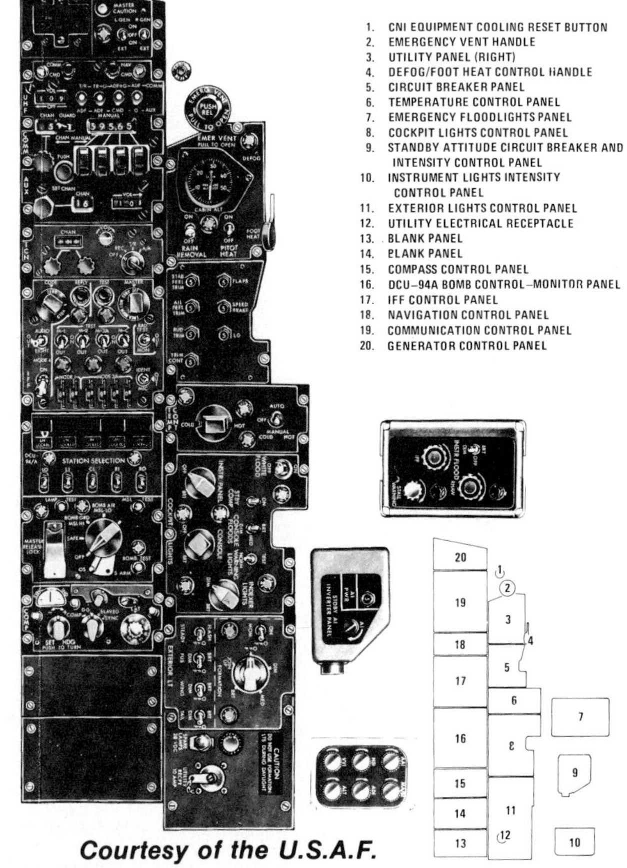

Courtesy of the U.S.A.F.

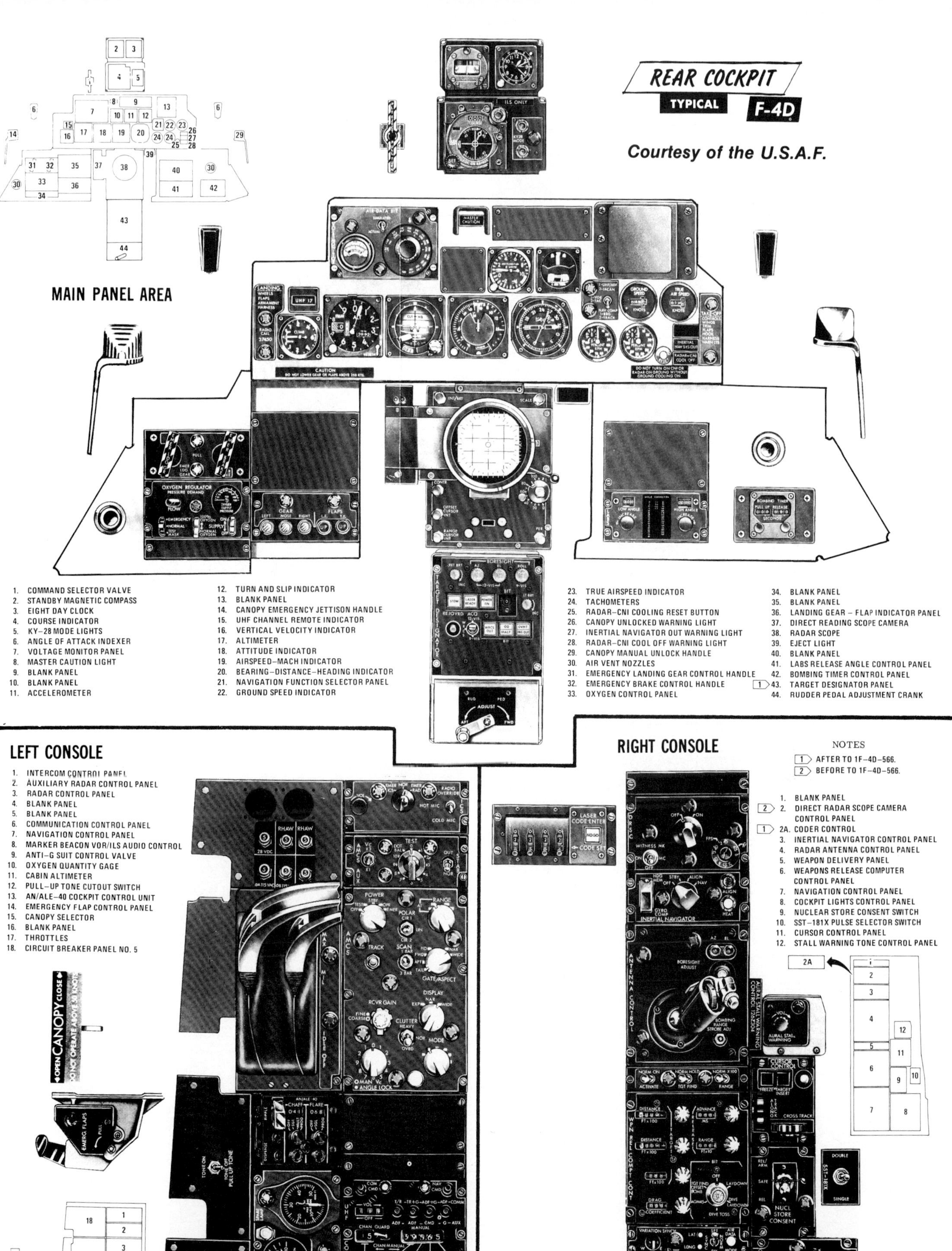
REAR COCKPIT
TYPICAL
F-4D
Courtesy of the U.S.A.F.
MAIN PANEL AREA
LEFT CONSOLE
RIGHT CONSOLE
NOTES
AFTER TO 1F-4D-566.
BEFORE TO 1F-4D-566.

1. COMMAND SELECTOR VALVE
2. STANDBY MAGNETIC COMPASS
3. EIGHT DAY CLOCK
4. COURSE INDICATOR
5. KY-28 MODE LIGHTS
6. ANGLE OF ATTACK INDEXER
7. VOLTAGE MONITOR PANEL
8. MASTER CAUTION LIGHT
9. BLANK PANEL
10. BLANK PANEL
11. ACCELEROMETER
12. TURN AND SLIP INDICATOR
13. BLANK PANEL
14. CANOPY EMERGENCY JETTISON HANDLE
15. UHF CHANNEL REMOTE INDICATOR
16. VERTICAL VELOCITY INDICATOR
17. ALTIMETER
18. ATTITUDE INDICATOR
19. AIRSPEED-MACH INDICATOR
20. BEARING-DISTANCE-HEADING INDICATOR
21. NAVIGATION FUNCTION SELECTOR PANEL
22. GROUND SPEED INDICATOR
23. TRUE AIRSPEED INDICATOR
24. TACHOMETERS
25. RADAR-CNI COOLING RESET BUTTON
26. CANOPY UNLOCKED WARNING LIGHT
27. INERTIAL NAVIGATOR OUT WARNING LIGHT
28. RADAR-CNI COOL OFF WARNING LIGHT
29. CANOPY MANUAL UNLOCK HANDLE
30. AIR VENT NOZZLES
31. EMERGENCY LANDING GEAR CONTROL HANDLE
32. EMERGENCY BRAKE CONTROL HANDLE
33. OXYGEN CONTROL PANEL
34. BLANK PANEL
35. BLANK PANEL
36. LANDING GEAR - FLAP INDICATOR PANEL
37. DIRECT READING SCOPE CAMERA
38. RADAR SCOPE
39. EJECT LIGHT
40. BLANK PANEL
41. LABS RELEASE ANGLE CONTROL PANEL
42. BOMBING TIMER CONTROL PANEL
43. TARGET DESIGNATOR PANEL
44. RUDDER PEDAL ADJUSTMENT CRANK

LEFT CONSOLE
1. INTERCOM CONTROL PANEL
2. AUXILIARY RADAR CONTROL PANEL
3. RADAR CONTROL PANEL
4. BLANK PANEL
5. BLANK PANEL
6. COMMUNICATION CONTROL PANEL
7. NAVIGATION CONTROL PANEL
8. MARKER BEACON VOR/ILS AUDIO CONTROL
9. ANTI-G SUIT CONTROL VALVE
10. OXYGEN QUANTITY GAGE
11. CABIN ALTIMETER
12. PULL-UP TONE CUTOUT SWITCH
13. AN/ALE-40 COCKPIT CONTROL UNIT
14. EMERGENCY FLAP CONTROL PANEL
15. CANOPY SELECTOR
16. BLANK PANEL
17. THROTTLES
18. CIRCUIT BREAKER PANEL NO. 5

RIGHT CONSOLE
1. BLANK PANEL
2. DIRECT RADAR SCOPE CAMERA CONTROL PANEL
2A. CODER CONTROL
3. INERTIAL NAVIGATOR CONTROL PANEL
4. RADAR ANTENNA CONTROL PANEL
5. WEAPON DELIVERY PANEL
6. WEAPONS RELEASE COMPUTER CONTROL PANEL
7. NAVIGATION CONTROL PANEL
8. COCKPIT LIGHTS CONTROL PANEL
9. NUCLEAR STORE CONSENT SWITCH
10. SST-181X PULSE SELECTOR SWITCH
11. CURSOR CONTROL PANEL
12. STALL WARNING TONE CONTROL PANEL

Nose gear from front. Note the taxi lights on the door, and the small antenna above the lights.
(Kunhert)

Nose gear from left. Note the torque link and oleo in this view.
(Kunhert)

RF-4C nose gear from front. Note the position of the lights and the blade antenna as compared to the photo above. This is the only difference in landing gear detail among the F-4C, F-4D and RF-4C versions.
(Spidle)

Nose gear well detail.

Right main landing gear detail. Note the clamp over the oleo to prevent the gear from collapsing while the aircraft is on the ground.

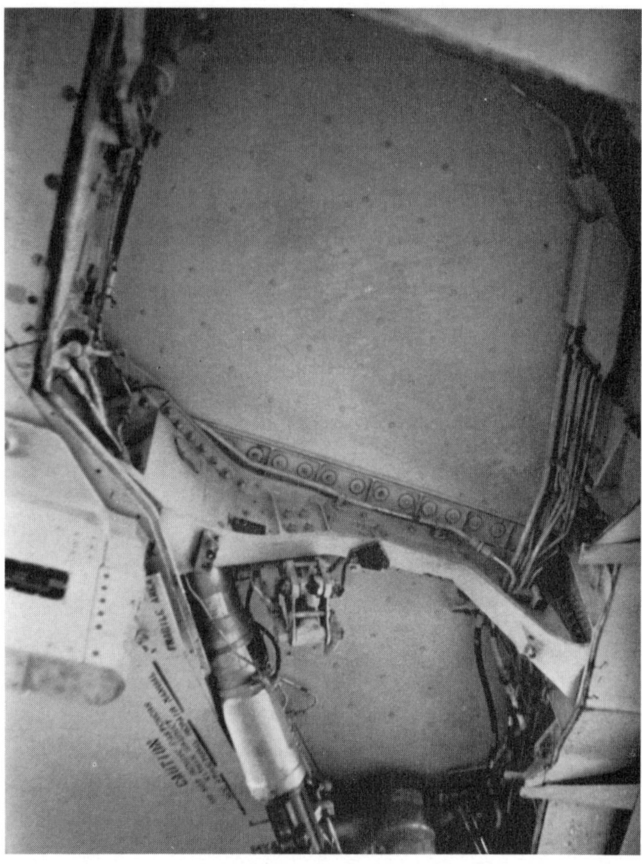

Right main gear well looking out toward the main strut.

Left main gear detail. Note the tie-down loop above the oleo.

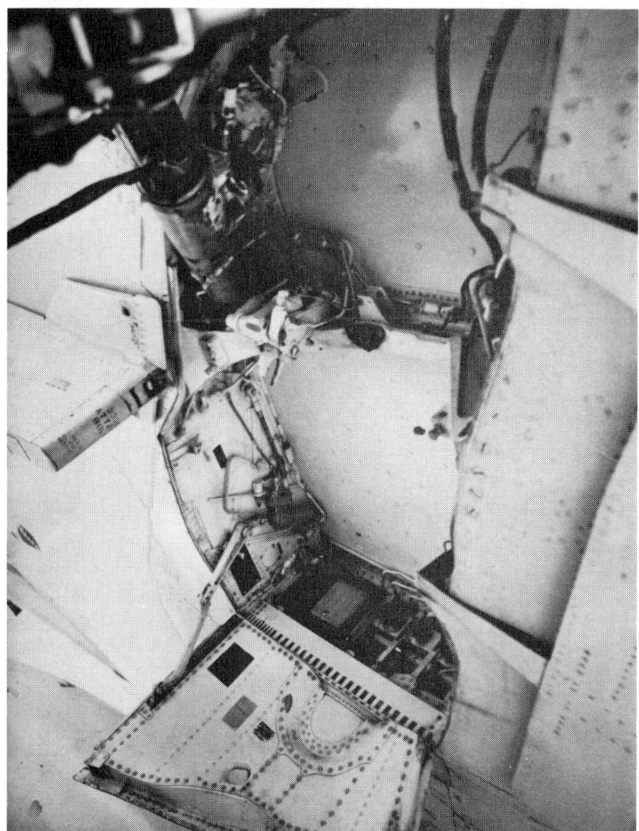

Left main gear well looking in toward the fuselage. Note how close the trailing edge of the inboard pylon is to the edge of the well.

MARTIN-BAKER EJECTION SEAT DETAIL

NOTES

■1 SEATS EQUIPPED WITH REMOVABLE DROGUE PARACHUTE PACK ASSEMBLY

■2 63-7740 THRU 67-469 BEFORE T.O. 1F-4-832

■3 68-548 AND UP; ALSO 63-7740 THRU 67-469 AFTER T.O. 1F-4-832

■4 AFTER T.O. 1F-4-926

■5 63-7740 THRU 69-384 BEFORE T.O. 1F-4-898

■6 71-248 AND UP; ALSO 63-7740 THRU 69-384 AFTER T.O. 1F-4-898

■7 63-7740 THRU 71-254

■8 71-255 AND UP; ALSO ON 63-7740 THRU 71-254,

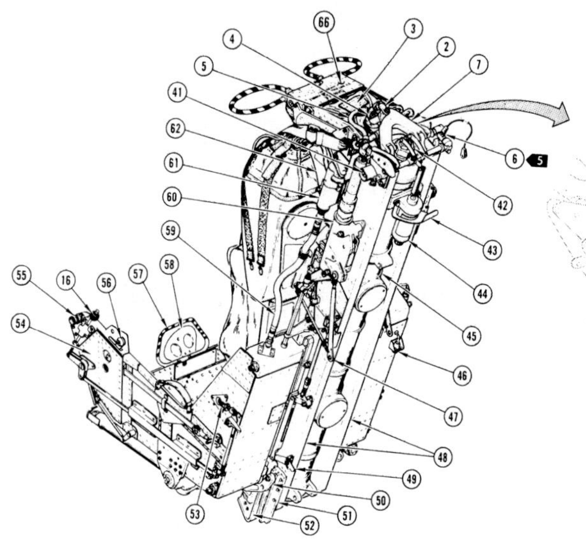

INDEX NO.	NOMENCLATURE
1	DROGUE PARACHUTE PACK ASSEMBLY
2	DROGUE SHACKLE
3	DROGUE PARACHUTE
4	RELEASE ASSEMBLY LINE
5	DROGUE WITHDRAWAL LINE
6	CANOPY INTERLOCK BLOCK
7	SCISSORS MECHANISM
8	FACE CURTAIN HANDLE
9	PERSONNEL PARACHUTE BACKREST
10	GAS POWERED INERTIA REEL
11	SEAT BUCKET POSITIONING ACTUATOR
12	EMERGENCY OXYGEN CYLINDER
13	STICKER CLIP
14	SEAT BUCKET HANDLE
15	SEAT BUCKET POSITIONING SWITCH
16	EMERGENCY OXYGEN MANUAL RELEASE CONTROL HANDLE
17	PERSONNEL PARACHUTE SPRINGS
18	PERSONNEL PARACHUTE
19	PERSONNEL PARACHUTE CONTAINER HOLDDOWN STRAP
20	PERSONNEL PARACHUTE WITHDRAWAL LINE
21	LUMBAR PAD
22	LUMBAR PAD ATTACHMENT STRAP
■7 23	LEG GUARD PLATE-WINGED IN FWD COCKPIT-STRAIGHT IN AFT COCKPIT
■8 23A	LEG GUARD PLATE-NO WING
24	FINGER TAB
25	ROCKET MOTOR

INDEX NO.	NOMENCLATURE
26	ROCKET NOZZLES PROTECTIVE COVER
27	ROCKET MOTOR FIRING LANYARD AND DISPENSER
28	ROCKET MOTOR FIRING MECHANISM PROTECTIVE BOOT
29	ROCKET MOTOR FIRING MECHANISM
30	LEG RESTRAINT ASSEMBLY
31	LEG RESTRAINT CORD ANCHOR
32	LEG RESTRAINT CORD ROLLER
33	GUILLOTINE FIRING MECHANISM
34	EMERGENCY HARNESS RELEASE HANDLE
35	INERTIA REEL GAS LINE AND QUICK DISCONNECT COUPLING
36	SEAT BUCKET QUICK RELEASE PIN
37	TIME RELEASE MECHANISM TRIP ROD
38	SEAT ACTUATOR ELECTRICAL DISCONNECT (SEAT BUCKET TO ACTUATOR)
39	PERSONNEL PARACHUTE RESTRAINT STRAP
40	TIME RELEASE MECHANISM
41	TOP LATCH MECHANISM
42	CATAPULT GUN FIRING MECHANISM
43	FIRING MECHANISM GUARD (FORWARD SEAT)
44	SEAT MOUNTED INITIATOR
45	CATAPULT GUN
46	SEAT ACTUATOR ELECTRICAL DISCONNECT (SEAT BUCKET TO AIRCRAFT)
47	DROGUE GUN TRIP ROD
48	MAIN BEAM ASSEMBLY
49	LOWER EJECTION MECHANISM FIRING LINK
50	ROCKET MOTOR THRUST ANGLE ADJUSTMENT ARM
51	ROCKET MOTOR GUIDE TRACK
52	SEAT BUCKET GUIDE TRACK
53	EMERGENCY OXYGEN LANYARD DISCONNECT
54	SEAT BUCKET
55	LEG RESTRAINT MANUAL RELEASE HANDLE
56	SHOULDER HARNESS MANUAL CONTROL HANDLE
57	LOWER EJECTION HANDLE
58	LOWER EJECTION HANDLE GUARD
59	GUILLOTINE GAS LINE
60	DROGUE GUN
61	GUILLOTINE KNIFE BLADE ASSEMBLY
62	DROGUE CONTAINER
63	D-RING AND PLATE
64	CANOPY INTERLOCK BLOCK AND CATAPULT GUN FIRING MECHANISM (INTERDICTOR) SAFETY PIN ASSEMBLY
65	FIRING MECHANISM GUARD (AFT SEAT)
66	ROCKET ASSIST EJECTION SEAT

Courtesy of the U.S.A.F.

F-4C & F-4D DETAILS

IR sensor on an F-4C. *(Kunhert)*

IR sensor on an F-4D. Note the bulge on the rear half of the sensor. This difference in IR sensors is about the only noticeable external difference between the F-4C and F-4D. *(Thurlow)*

Windscreen detail on an F-4D. The small hole just in front of the windscreen is a blower vent that removes rain from the center part of the windscreen.

Rear canopy detail. Note the external mirror on the center framing. This is an aid to help the rear seater "check six".

Horizontal stabilizer detail. F-4C's, F-4D's and RF-4C's were not retro-fitted with the slotted leading edges on the horizontal stabilizers that became standard on the F-4E. Navy F-4B's and F-4N's were retro-fitted. *(Kunhert)*

Forward left AIM-7 Sparrow bay. Note also the bleed air vents.

Forward right AIM-7 Sparrow bay.

Open speed brake detail under left wing. Right side brake is the same. Inner brake panel is red.

One of two auxilliary air intake doors located on either side of the centerline station. Door is opened to provide extra air to the engine at slow speeds, and opens whenever the landing gear is lowered. Doors are usually open when the aircraft is on the ground.

Leading edge flaps on an F-4D. These are the same for the F-4C, F-4D, and RF-4C. Early F-4E's also had this arrangement, but later the F-4E was fitted with "maneuvering slats" and a small boundary layer fence.

Raised spoiler on top of left wing.   *(Leader)*

PYLON DETAILS

Originally the inboard pylons on Air Force Phantoms were the same as the ones on Navy F-4's. This pylon had a straight leading edge, and is still seen on many RF-4C's.

The Navy style inboard pylon was replaced with a new style as shown here. This pylon has a rounded leading edge. Note the anti-sway braces near the front and rear of the pylon.

Right inboard pylon with triple ejector rack (TER) attached. The TER permits three bombs, instead of just one, to be carried by the pylon. Note the extensive amount of stenciling on the pylon.

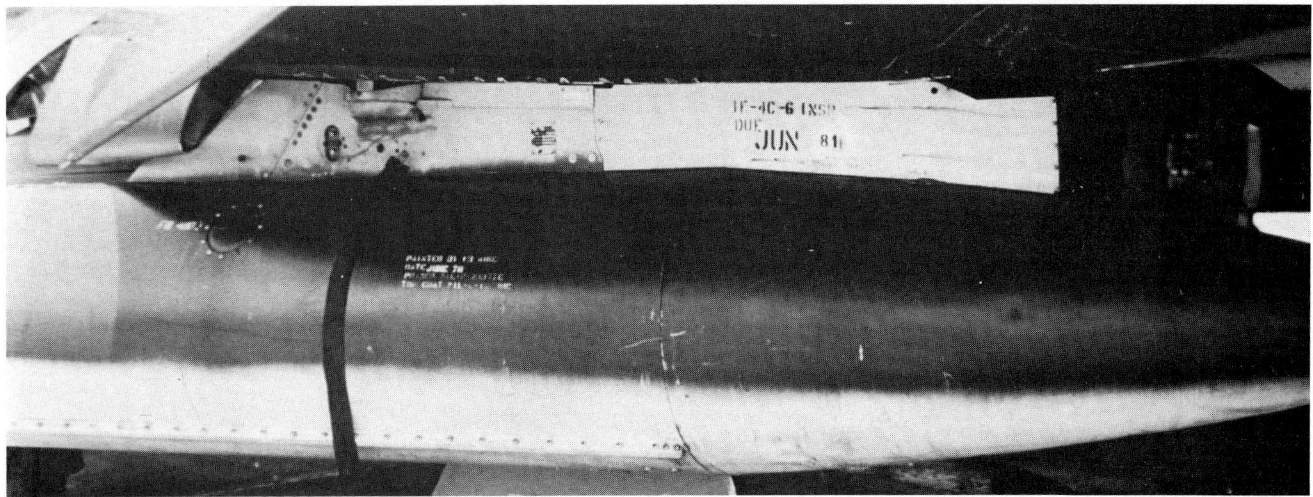

Outboard pylon with fuel tank attached. Note the small gap between the pylon and the wing at the trailing end. Also note the anti-sway brace near the front of the pylon.

(Leader)

F-4C & F-4D ARMAMENT

"DUMB BOMBS"

In-flight bomb check close-up of an F-4D en route to target. Bombs on the inboard pylons have fuse extenders while those on the centerline do not. Note the lack of AIM-7's and the ECM pod in the forward left Sparrow bay. Photo was taken on a flight out of Udorn in 1973. (Thurlow)

MK-82, 500 pound low drag bombs on a triple ejector rack (TER) attached to the left inboard pylon on an F-4D. (France)

MK-82 (Snakeye) high drag 500 pound bombs on F-4C. Note the AIM-9 missile rail attached to the side of the pylon.

M117, 750 pound bombs ready for their targets in Vietnam. (Thurlow)

MK-83, 1000 pound bombs on an F-4D at Ubon, RTAB in 1973 (Thurlow)

VULCAN 20MM CANNON POD

Vulcan gun pod on centerline station of an F-4C. The biggest shortcoming of the F-4C and -D was its lack of an internal gun. Gun pods were only a partial answer since they were not as accurate as an internal gun, and they caused drag and thereby reduced aircraft performance.

Left side view of gun pod.

Open access panel on right side of gun pod showing ammunition feed system. Note vents for exhaust gases from ammunition being fired.

(Lloyd)

Pave Spike laser designator in the forward left Sparrow missile bay on an F-4D. (Leavitt)

MK-84 Laser Guided Bomb (LGB) on an F-4D at Udorn RTAB. (Thurlow)

MK-84 Electro-optical guided bomb attached to the outboard right pylon of an F-4. These bombs are known as Hobos. (Munkasy)

AGM-65 Maverick missile trainer on a triple launch rack. The training Maverick does not have the rear guidance fins of the actual missile. (France)

Two Maverick electro-optically (TV) guided missiles on left inboard pylon. Note the rear fins. Up to three missiles can be carried on the triple launch rack (Munkasy)

SUU-20 practice dispenser. Practice bombs can be carried on the rings inside this dispenser, and practice rockets can be fired from the tubes mounted on the sides. This permits crew training without having to use full size and more expensive practice bombs.   *(Lloyd)*

AIM-9J Sidewinders shoulder mounted on the inboard right pylon of an F-4D. This arrangement allows more ordnance or other equipment to be carried beneath the pylon. In this photo an ALQ-71 ECM pod is fitted.   *(Thurlow)*

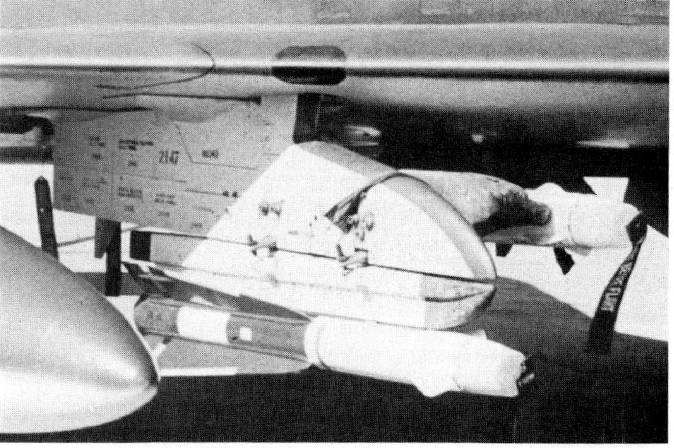

AIM-4D Falcon air-to-air missiles on the inboard pylon. This mounting prevented further use of the pylon for other stores while the missiles were in place. Falcons did not have proximity fuses like the Sidewinders, and required a direct hit on one of the fuses. The fuses are the white strips on the leading edge of the fins.   *(Munkasy)*

BDU-38 "shape" which simulates a nuclear weapon. All Air Force F-4's are nuclear capable, but in the case of the RF-4C, the weapon can only be carried on the centerline station.   *(Thurlow)*

NOTE: Pages 29 thru 32 show only a small sample of the most common external stores carried by the F-4C and F-4D. Complete coverage of the armament carried by the Phantom would fill several volumes, and is beyond the scope of this publication.

F-4C, 63-685, of the 57th FIS as seen at the 1976 William Tell competition. Note the colors on the apple and the arrow. The black design behind the arrow is a map of Iceland with "57 FIS" in white. The map of Iceland replaced a former design that featured a knight with a lance chasing a bear with a red star. This former design was featured on F-102 aircraft flown previously by the 57 FIS. Checkerboard designs are on the vertical tail, outer portions of the horizontal stabilizers, and on the forward nose gear door under the lights. A photo of another aircraft from this unit taken at William Tell, 1976 appears on the cover of this book.   *(Leader)*

F-4C, 63-576. Personal aircraft of the commander of the Air Defense Weapons Center. Note the stripes on the splitter plate, and that the stripes on the fuel tanks are on both sides of each tank.   *(Campbell)*

F-4C COCKPIT

Front instrument panel in F-4C. Note the radar scope at the top of the panel and the gunsight glass just under the windscreen.

Rear instrument panel in F-4C. Note the mirrors on the inside of the cockpit. The rear cockpit contains only basic flying instruments as compared to the front cockpit.

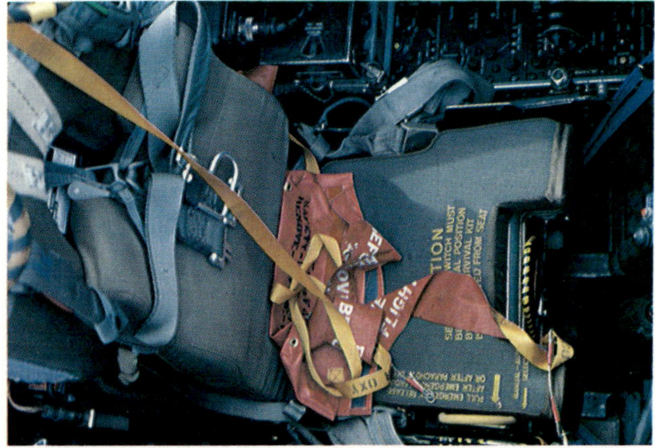

Looking down on seat and survival pack. Note the brown color of the seat back as compared to the olive green color of the survival pack. Note also the yellow stenciling on the survival pack. (Leader)

Top of ejection seat showing rings for the face curtain and seat colors. In the F-4 the parachute pack normally stays in the aircraft as shown here.

F-4D COCKPIT

Front instrument panel in F-4D

Close-up of control column and center console in F-4D.

Rear instrument panel in F-4D.

Rear cockpit in F-4D. Note the circuit breaker panels on the fuselage side.

MiG KILLER

F-4C, 64-0660, as seen at Luke AFB in September 1979. MiG kill markings remain painted on the splitter plate indicating successful combat in the skies over Vietnam.

(Bossie)

Close-up of the MiG kill markings on 64-0660. This photo was enlarged to this size to clearly show the three red stars, each indicating a MiG-17 kill. The small stenciling under each star indicates the dates on which the kills were made. From top to bottom, the kills were made on 12 May, 1966, 14 May, 1967, and 3 June, 1967.

(Bossie)

F-4 D RADAR

Shown here are two views of the radar in the F-4D. The radome opens to the right, folding back along the side of the fuselage. Then the radar slides out on rails for easy access. Photos and drawings exist of an F-4D with a flat radar antenna, but in that case the F-4 was being used as a test bed for the F-16 radar.

RF-4C

The first prototype RF-4C on roll-out from the plant. Note the long boom attached to the nose. The first six RF-4C's were converted Navy F-4B's and had the thin tires. (McDonnell Douglas)

RF-4C of the 106th TRS. Note the "wrap-around" camouflage scheme on this aircraft. (Leader)

All white and red RF-4C, 65-0905, at Hill AFB, Utah, November 20, 1976 (Knowles via Leader)

RF-4C DETAILS

Front instrument panel in RF-4C. (Leader)

Rear instrument panel in RF-4C. (Leader)

RF-4C radar from right side. (Leader)

RF-4C radar from front. (Leader)

Photoflash cartridge ejector open on left rear of aircraft (Leader)

KA-56 still picture camera on open door. (Leader)

F-4D, 66-617, of the 49th TFW at Holloman AFB in March, 1976. Aircraft has white stenciling over the green areas and black stenciling over the tan and the light gray undersurfaces. This is standard whenever white stenciling is used on camouflaged aircraft.

F-4C, 63-7424, in overall white with red markings. Photo taken at Hill AFB, Utah in July, 1980.

F-4C, 63-7407, in overall gray scheme as seen on November 4, 1976. This aircraft belongs to the Air Force Systems Command.

(Leader)

F-4C, F-4D, RF-4C DIMENSIONS

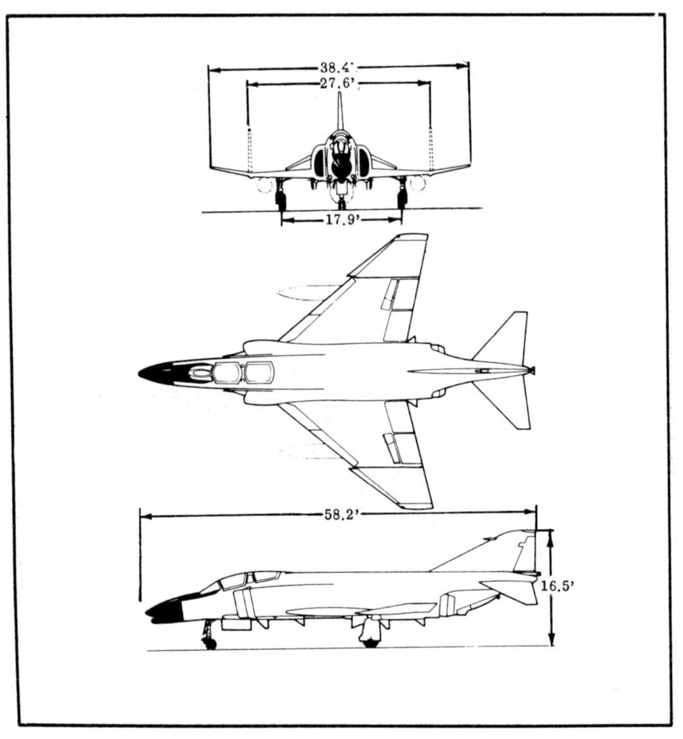

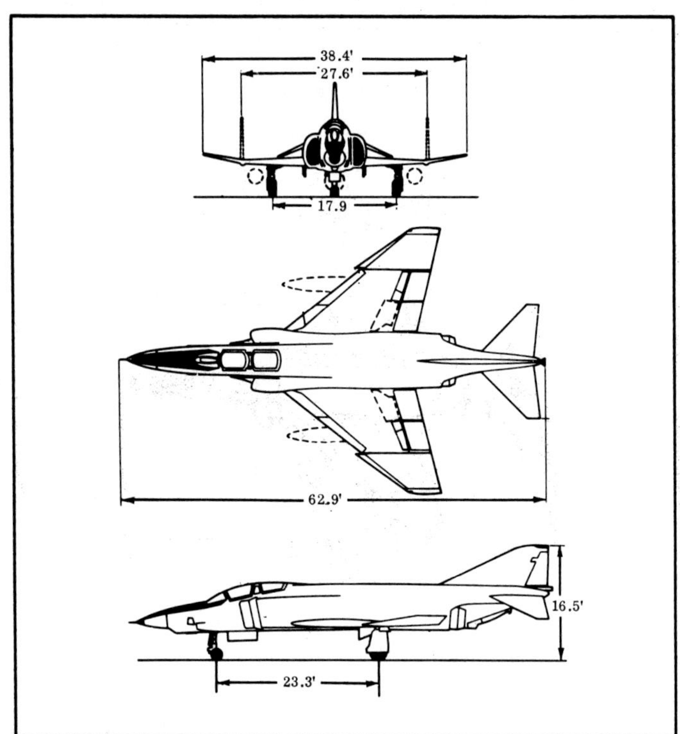

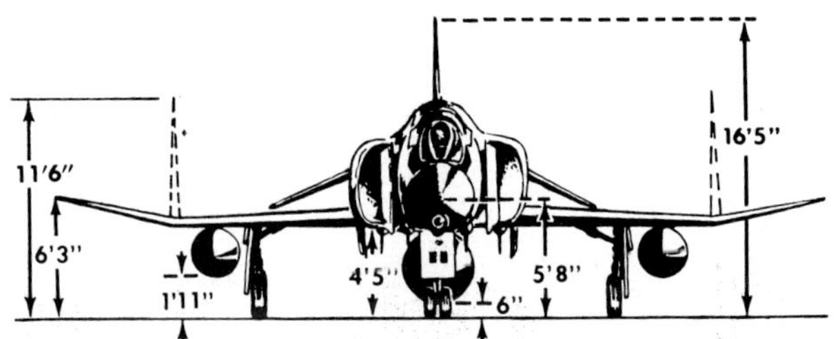

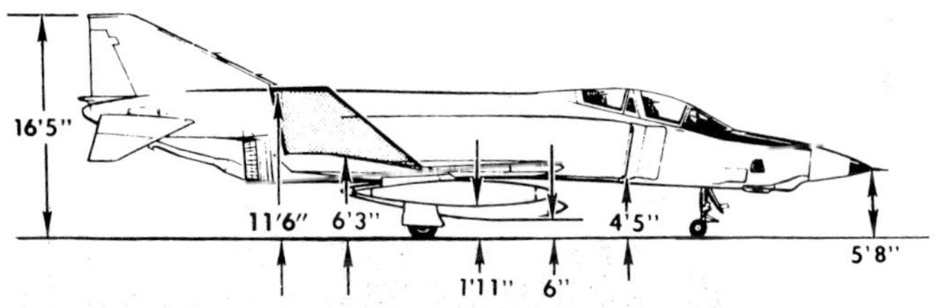

Courtesy of the U.S.A.F.

DIMENSION DATA

DIMENSION	ACTUAL	1/72nd SCALE	1/48th SCALE	1/32nd SCALE
LENGTH (F-4C/D)	58.2'	9.70"	14.55"	21.83"
LENGTH (RF-4C)	62.9'	10.48"	15.73"	23.59"
WINGSPAN	38.4'	6.40"	9.60"	14.40"
WINGS FOLDED	27.6'	4.60"	6.90"	10.35"
HEIGHT	16.5'	2.75"	4.13"	6.19"
WHEEL TREAD	17.9'	2.98"	4.48"	6.71"
WHEEL TRACK	23.3'	3.88"	5.83"	8.74"

WING DATA:

```
Incidence ....................................................... 1°
Dihedral (Inner Panel) .......................................... 0°
Dihedral (Outer Panel) ......................................... 12°
Sweepback (25% chord) .......................................... 45°
Area ...................................................... 530 sq. ft.
Aspect Ratio ................................................... 2.82
M.A.C. ..................................................... 16.04 ft.
Wing Section (Parallel to Center Line)
    Root ............................................ NACA 0006.4-64 (Mod)
    Fold ............................................ NACA 0004-64 (Mod)
    Tip ............................................. NACA 0003-64 (Mod)
```

F-4C/D 1/72nd SCALE DRAWINGS

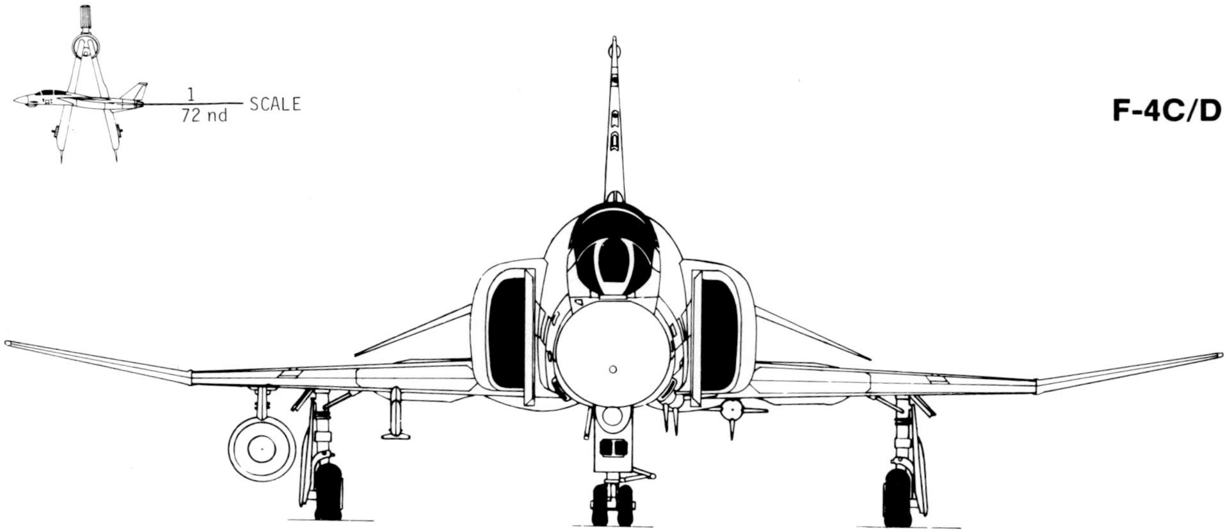

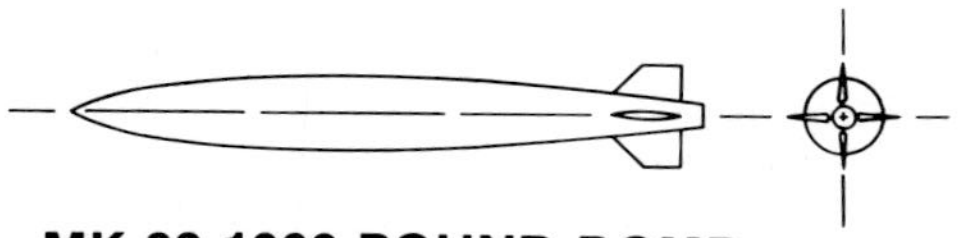

MK 83 1000 POUND BOMB

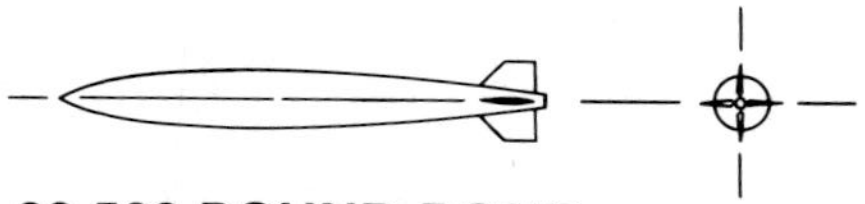

MK 82 500 POUND BOMB

Jerry G. Smith

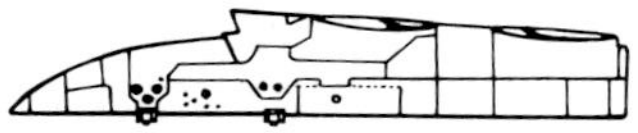

INBOARD PYLON

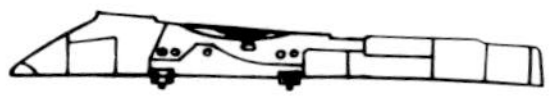

OUTBOARD PYLON

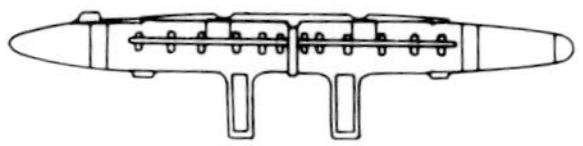

ALQ-87 ECM POD

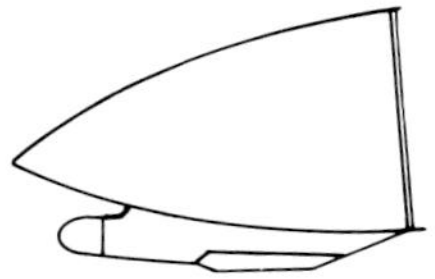

IR SENSOR
FOR F-4D

LORAN ANTENNA

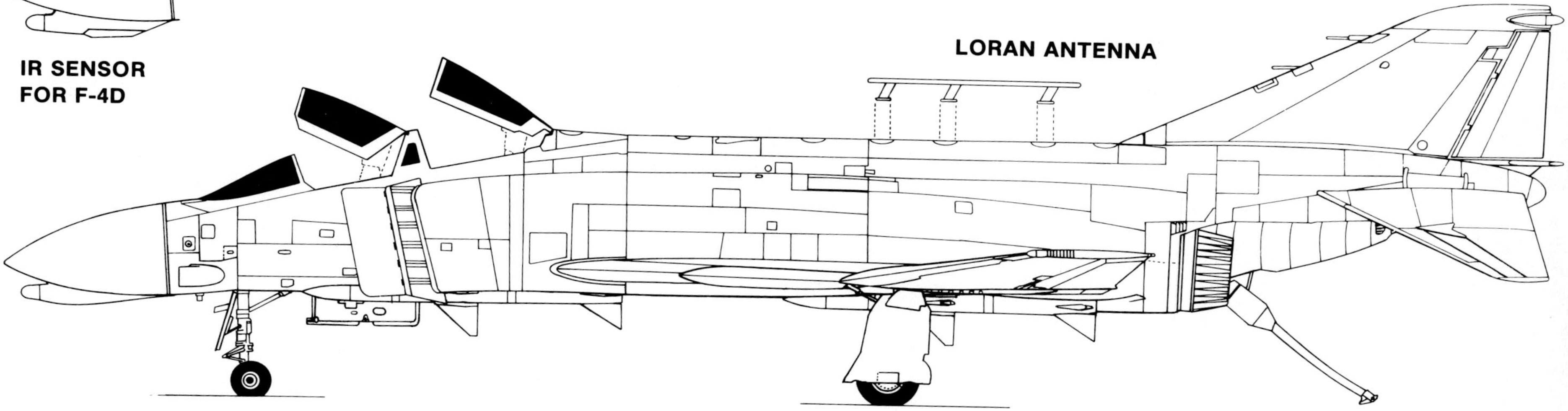

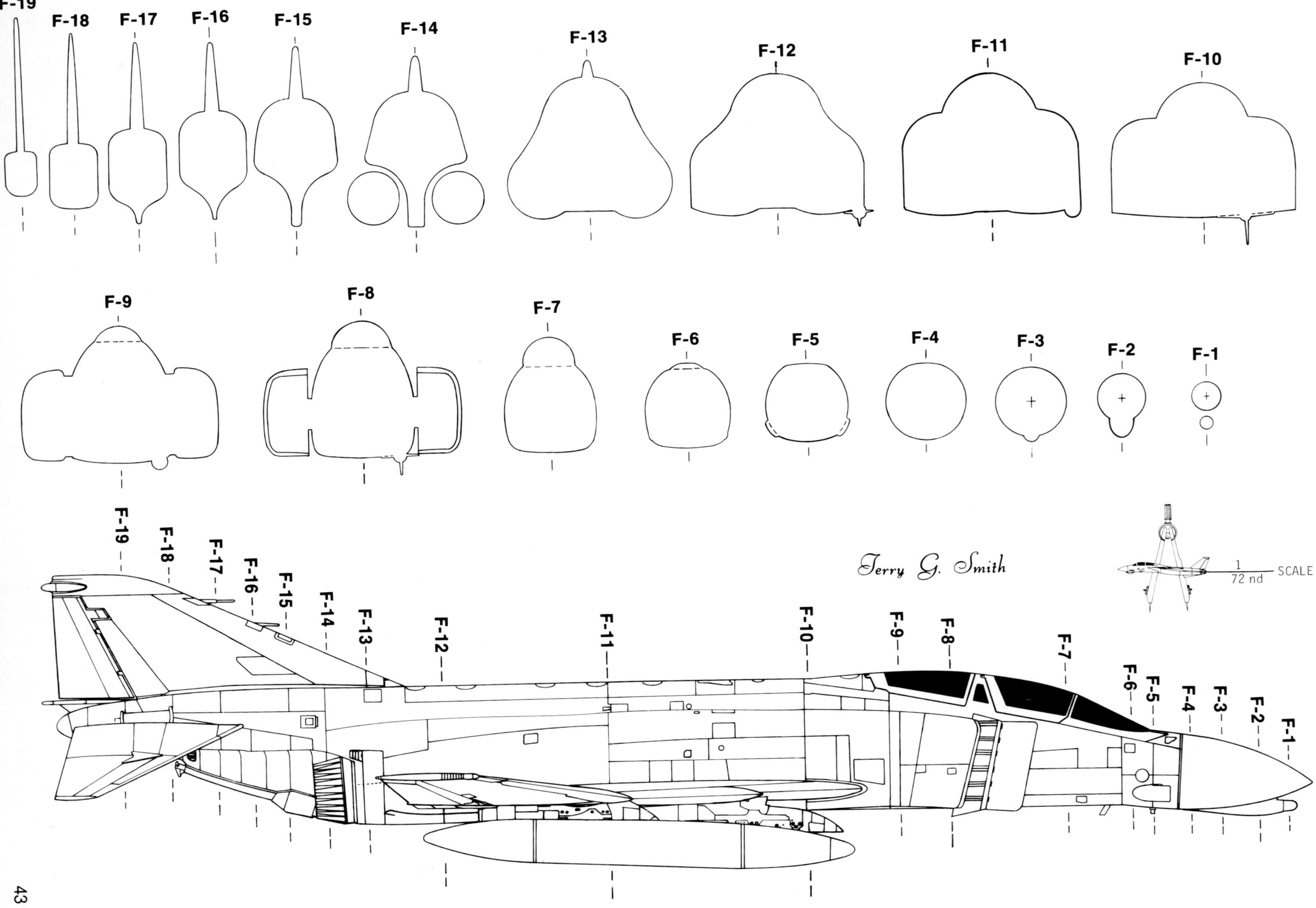

F-19
F-18
F-17
F-16
F-15
F-14
F-13
F-12
F-11
F-10
F-9
F-8
F-7
F-6
F-5
F-4
F-3
F-2
F-1
Jerry G. Smith
1
72 nd
SCALE

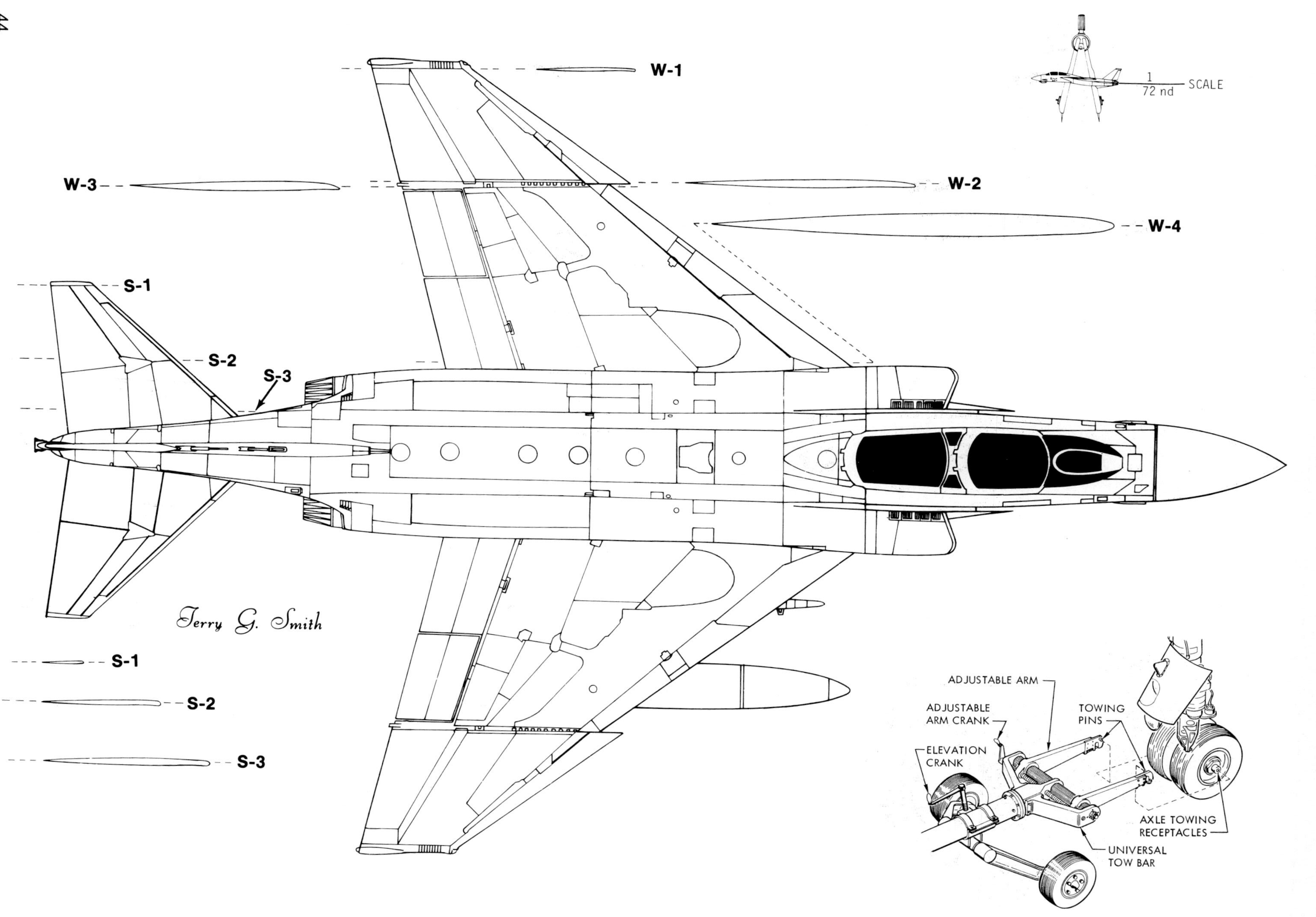
W-1
W-3
W-2
W-4
S-1
S-2
S-3
S-1
S-2
S-3
Terry G. Smith
SCALE
1
72 nd
ADJUSTABLE ARM
ADJUSTABLE ARM CRANK
ELEVATION CRANK
TOWING PINS
AXLE TOWING RECEPTACLES
UNIVERSAL TOW BAR

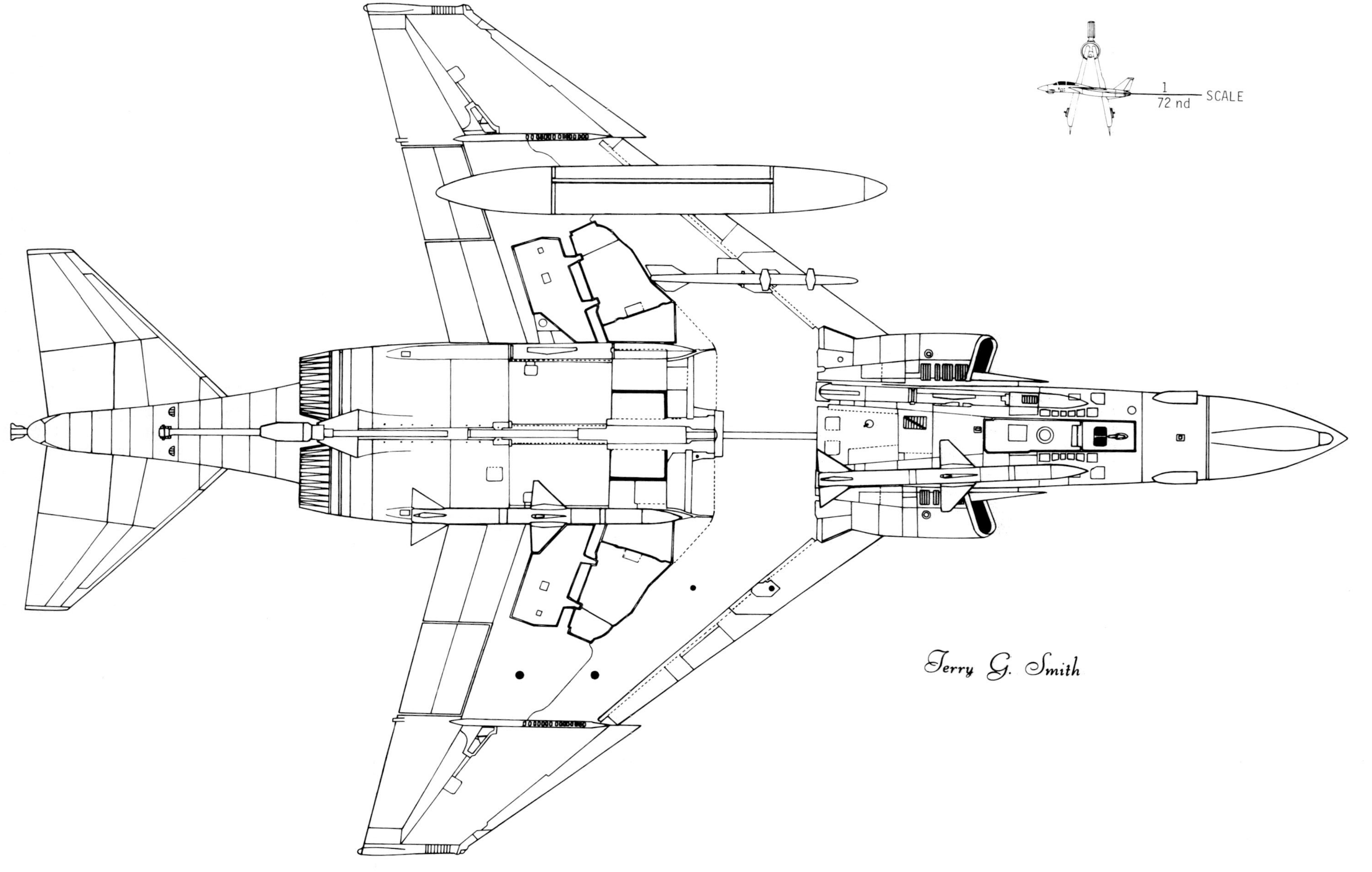

1
72 nd
SCALE
Jerry G. Smith

RF-4C 1/72nd SCALE DRAWINGS

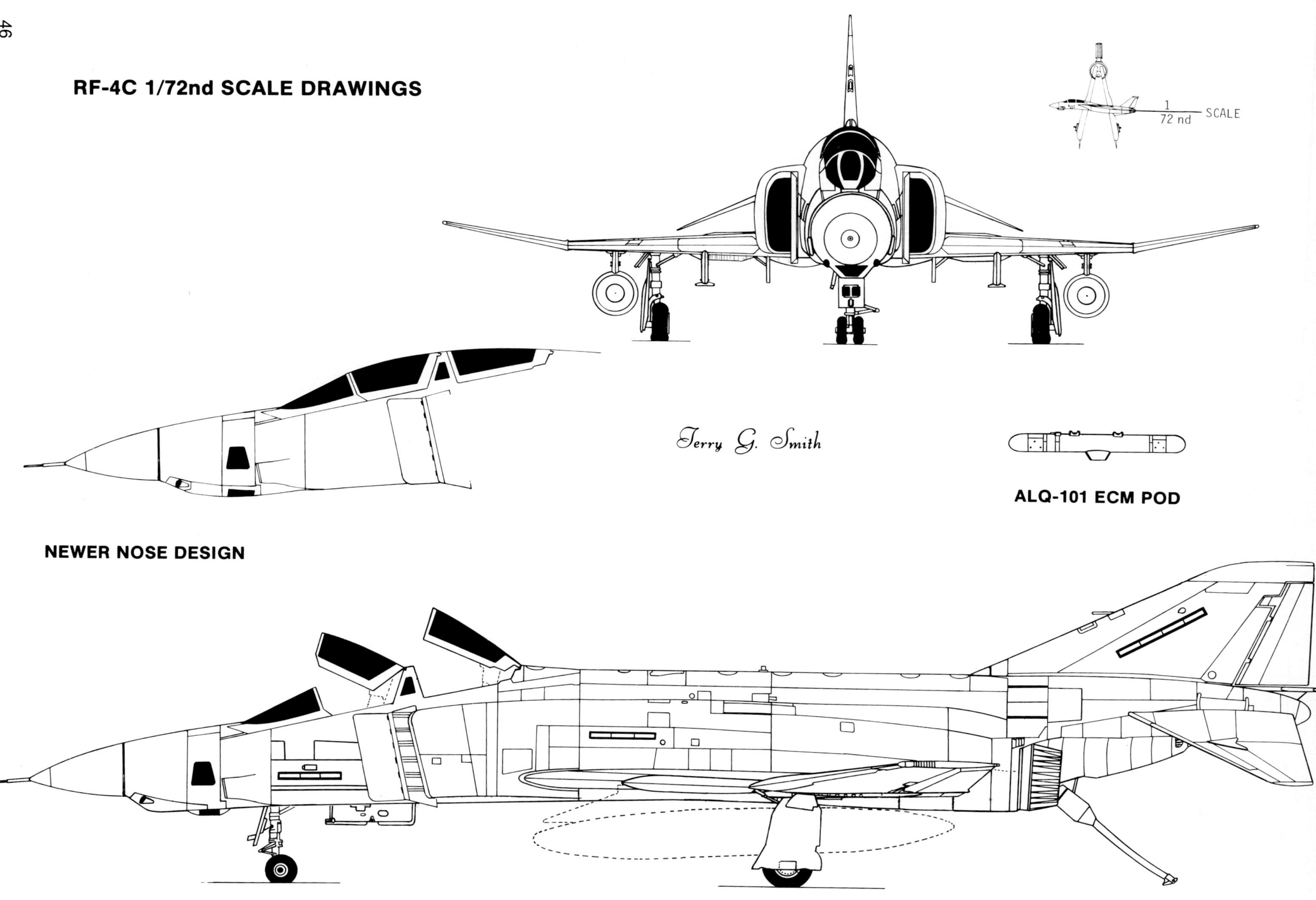

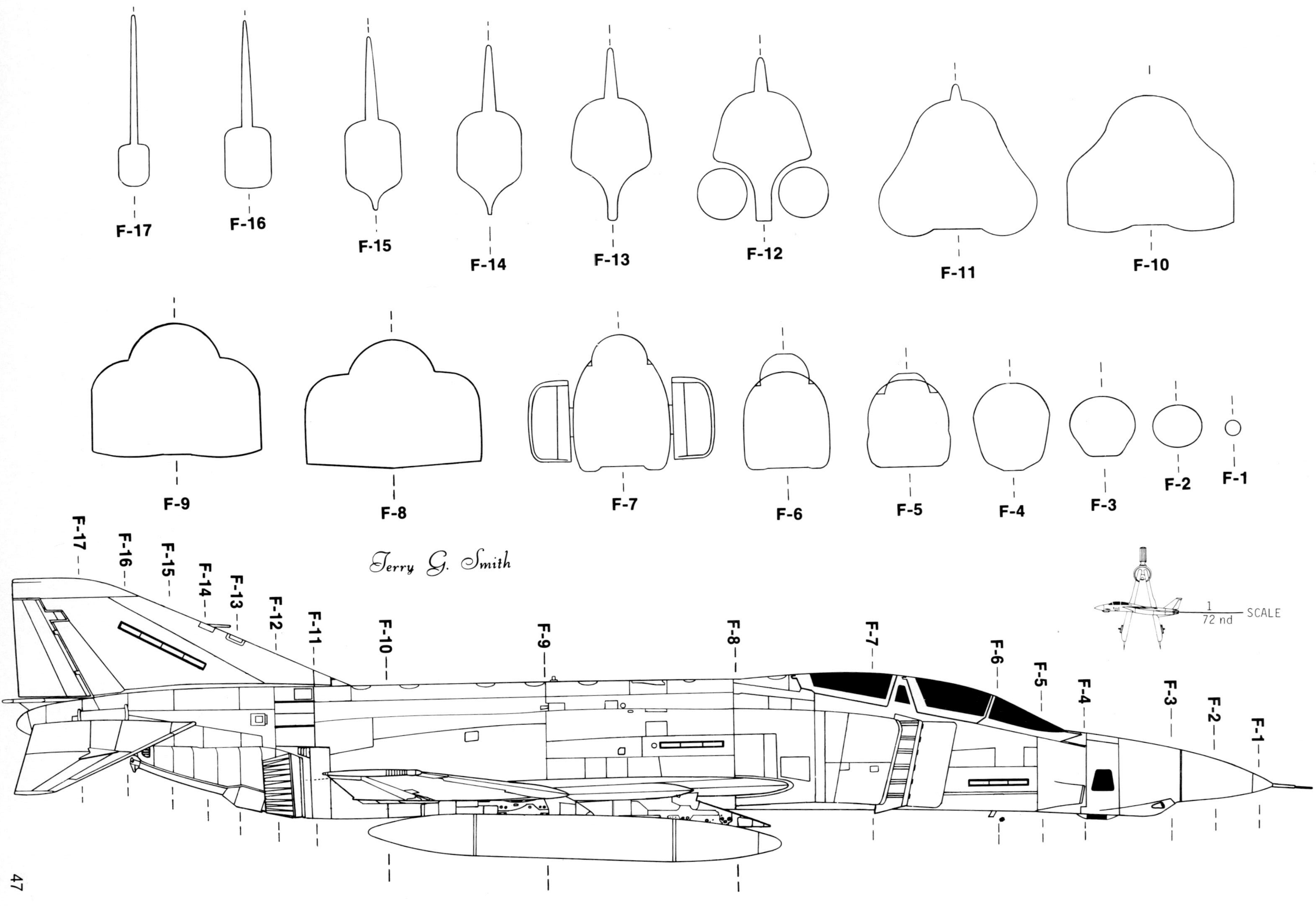

F-17
F-16
F-15
F-14
F-13
F-12
F-11
F-10
F-9
F-8
F-7
F-6
F-5
F-4
F-3
F-2
F-1
Jerry G. Smith
SCALE
1
72 nd

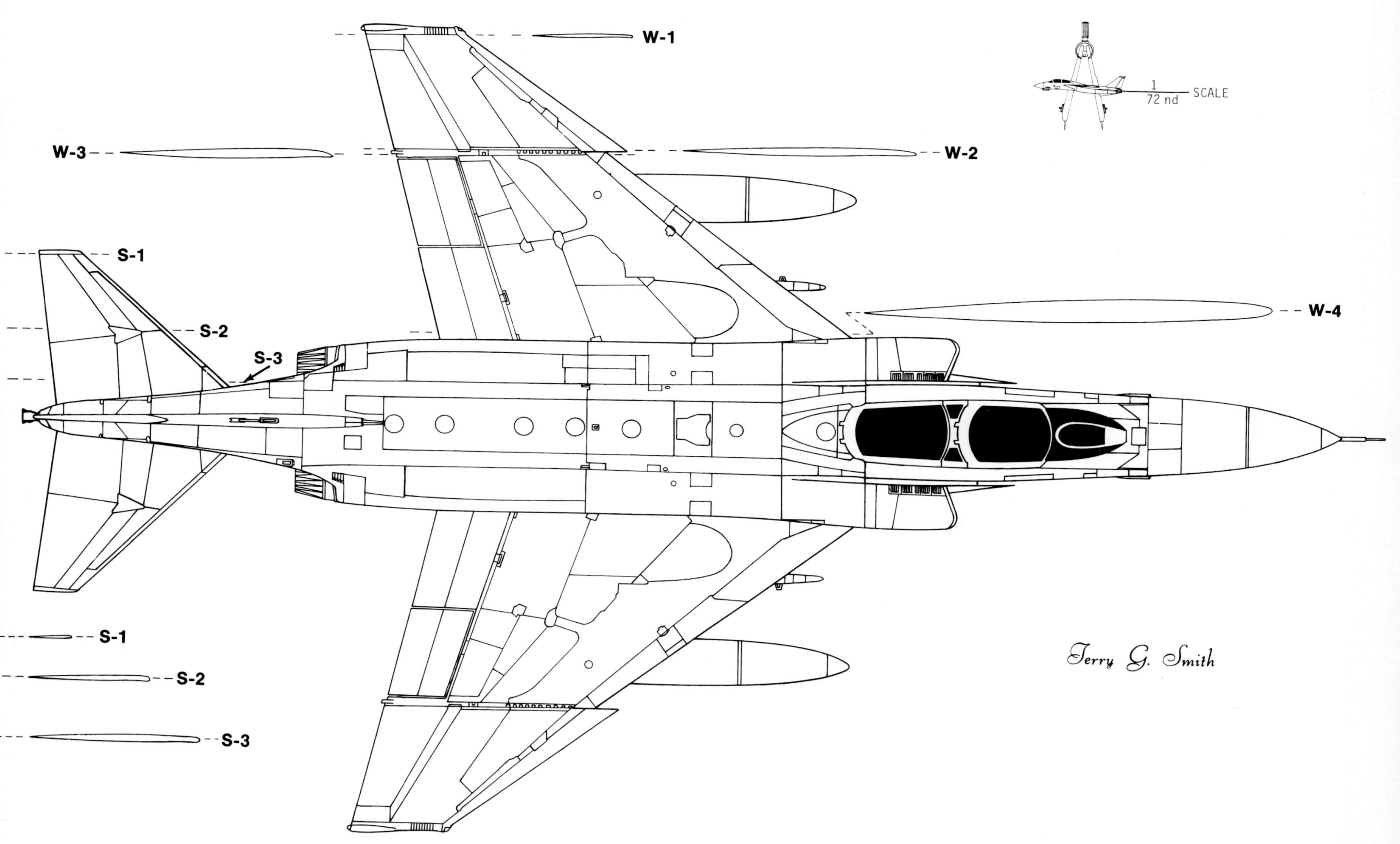
W-1
W-3
W-2
W-4
S-1
S-2
S-3
S-1
S-2
S-3
1
72 nd
SCALE
Jerry G. Smith

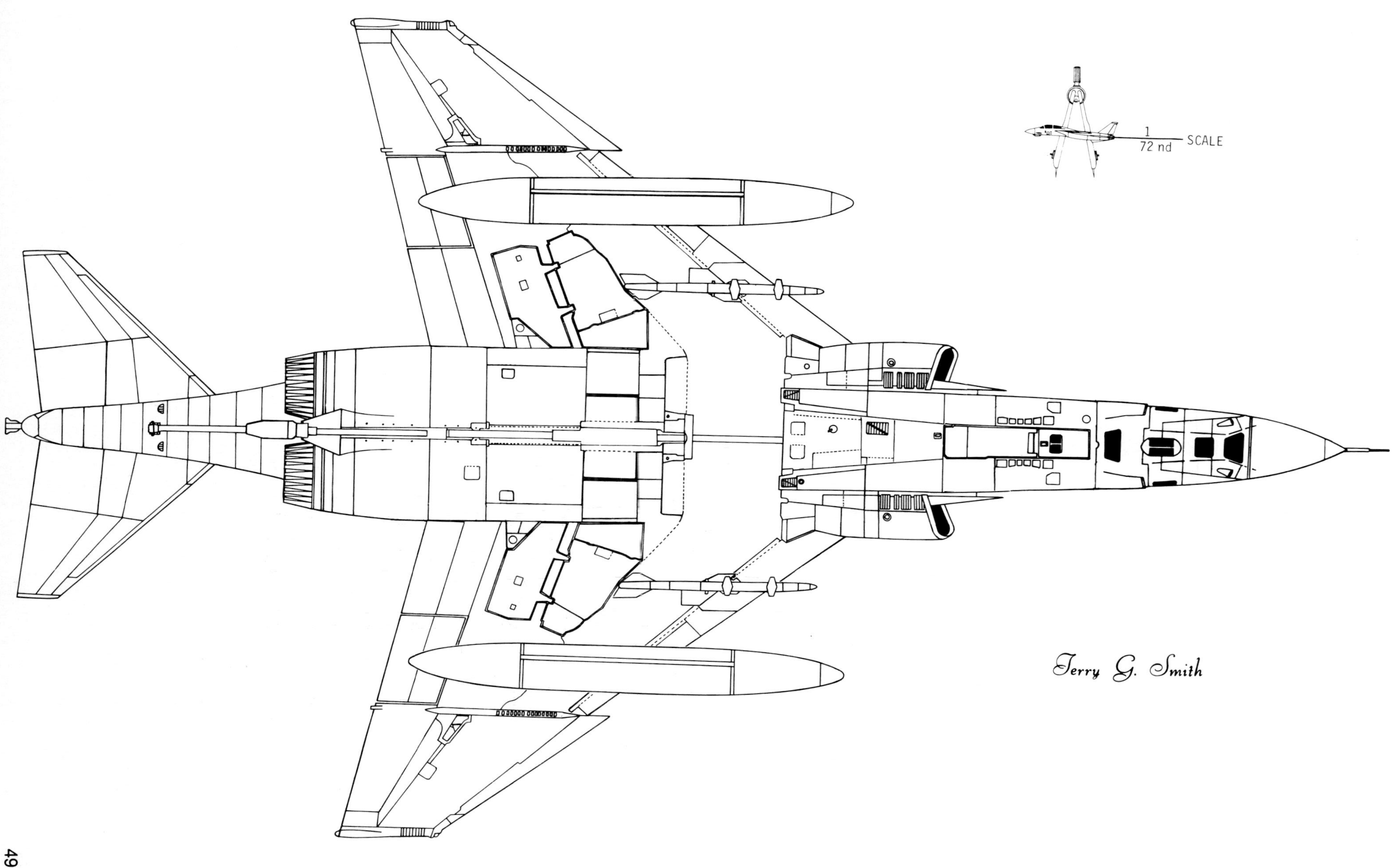

1
72 nd SCALE
Jerry G. Smith

RF-4C-26-MC, 65-881, of the 192nd TRS of the Nevada Air National Guard. Photo taken at Reno in October, 1976.
(Wilderdijk)

RF-4C DEVELOPMENT

As soon as the Air Force began its evaluation of Navy F-4B Phantoms they were impressed with its performance capabilities. Accordingly they started coming up with new roles and missions that this superb flying platform could perform. Among these was the role of tactical reconnaissance, and this resulted in Specific Operational Requirement (SOR) 196. This SOR was issued on May 29, 1962, only two months after the first contract had been issued for the basic F-4C. In fact, the SOR for the F-4C was not issued until August, 1962, after the requirements for the RF-4C. The SOR for the RF-4C also stipulated that the aircraft be able to deliver nuclear (but not conventional) weapons.

Six F-4B's were purchased from the Navy and converted on the assembly line to RF-4C test and evaluation aircraft. The first of these six aircraft made its maiden flight on August 8, 1963, twenty-three days ahead of schedule. The seventh RF-4C, which was the first production aircraft, made its first flight on May 18, 1964, about a month ahead of schedule. This aircraft, and all subsequent RF-4C's, had all of the changes incorporated on the F-4C including the wider tires and bulged wings.

Reconnaissance of Cuba in October, 1962, and in the early days of Vietnam had brought to light several deficiencies in reconnaissance equipment. This prompted the Air Force to make changes in the reconnaissance package that would be fitted into the RF-4C. As a result, the aircraft were ready before the reconnaissance equipment was, and the RF-4C entered service lacking fully qualified equipment.

Because of the situation in Southeast Asia, RF-4C's were rushed to the combat area on October 31, 1965. By late 1967 there were four squadrons in SEA, and they began replacing RF-101's in providing valuable reconnaissance information.

The RF-4C was much the same as its F-4C brother except for the obvious lengthened nose with its camera windows and other sensors. These sensors and cameras took up most of the room in the nose, and this meant that the radar for the RF-4C was the smaller AN/APQ-99. It could not guide the Sparrow missiles, so they were deleted. Their missile wells were covered over flush in the rear, and fairings replaced the forward two bays. Indeed no armament was to be carried by the RF-4C except for the nuclear weapons mentioned earlier. Other external stores are limited to fuel tanks, ECM pods, and a few reconnaissance pods.

It has been argued that the RF-4C could easily be fitted to carry four Sidewinders on its inboard pylons in the same manner as its fighting counterparts. The most often heard argument against providing the aircraft such self protection is that pilots might be tempted to "hassle" with enemy aircraft rather than "get in and get out" with their valuable intelligence information. Although it lacks defensive armament, the RF-4C is extensively equipped with defensive electronic countermeasures. But a former reconnaissance pilot once commented to the author about the phrase, "alone, unarmed, and unafraid," by saying, "Two out of three ain't bad!"

Prior to the RF-4, reconnaissance aircraft were usually nothing more than airplanes that carried cameras instead of guns. Both Navy and Air Force recon aircraft were limited primarily to relatively unsophisticated picture taking. The Phantom changed that dramatically. In addition to both high and low altitude photographic equipment, the RF-4C also has infrared, laser, and radar reconnaissance systems. The infrared system can detect hidden vehicles and other equipment by their heat signatures. One photo of a busy airport showed where airliners had recently been parked but had taxied away. Their shadows had left the ground

RADAR
100°
SCAN WIDTH
20°
SCAN WIDTH
SIDE LOOKING
RADAR

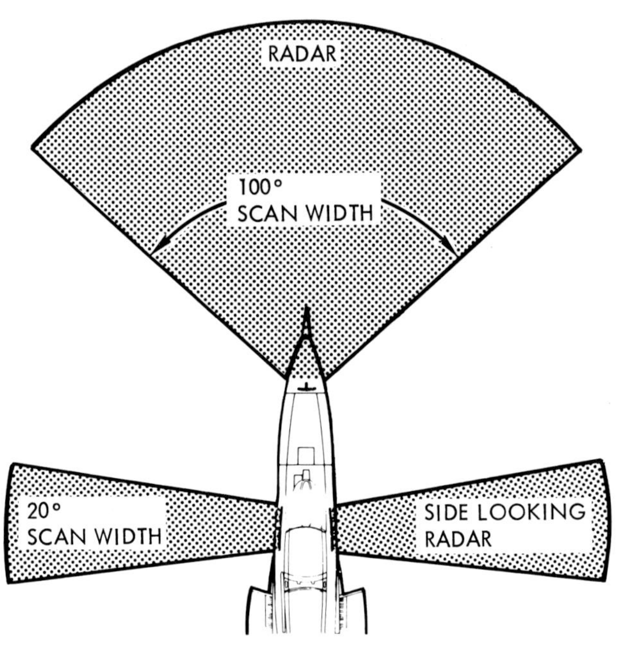

RADAR COVERAGE

beneath them cooler than the surrounding area! Also visible in the photo was an underground pipeline that was a different temperature than the ground covering it. These are but two examples of what IR reconnaissance can do that regular photography cannot do.

Radar reconnaissance is also quite remarkable. The side looking radar set (AN/APQ-102) has a moving target indicator (MTI) capability that can detect targets moving as slow as five knots at 90 degrees to the flight path. This MTI capability is based on a doppler shift generated by moving targets, and is very effective in locating moving trains, convoys, or armor formations.

Originally the RF-4C was able to eject a film cassette in flight to a user on the ground, however this system did not work out and the capability was dropped beginning with production block 44.

This multiple sensor system makes the RF-4 far more than a photo recon aircraft. It is a complete reconnaissance system capable of providing the Air Force with far greater capability than ever before possible.

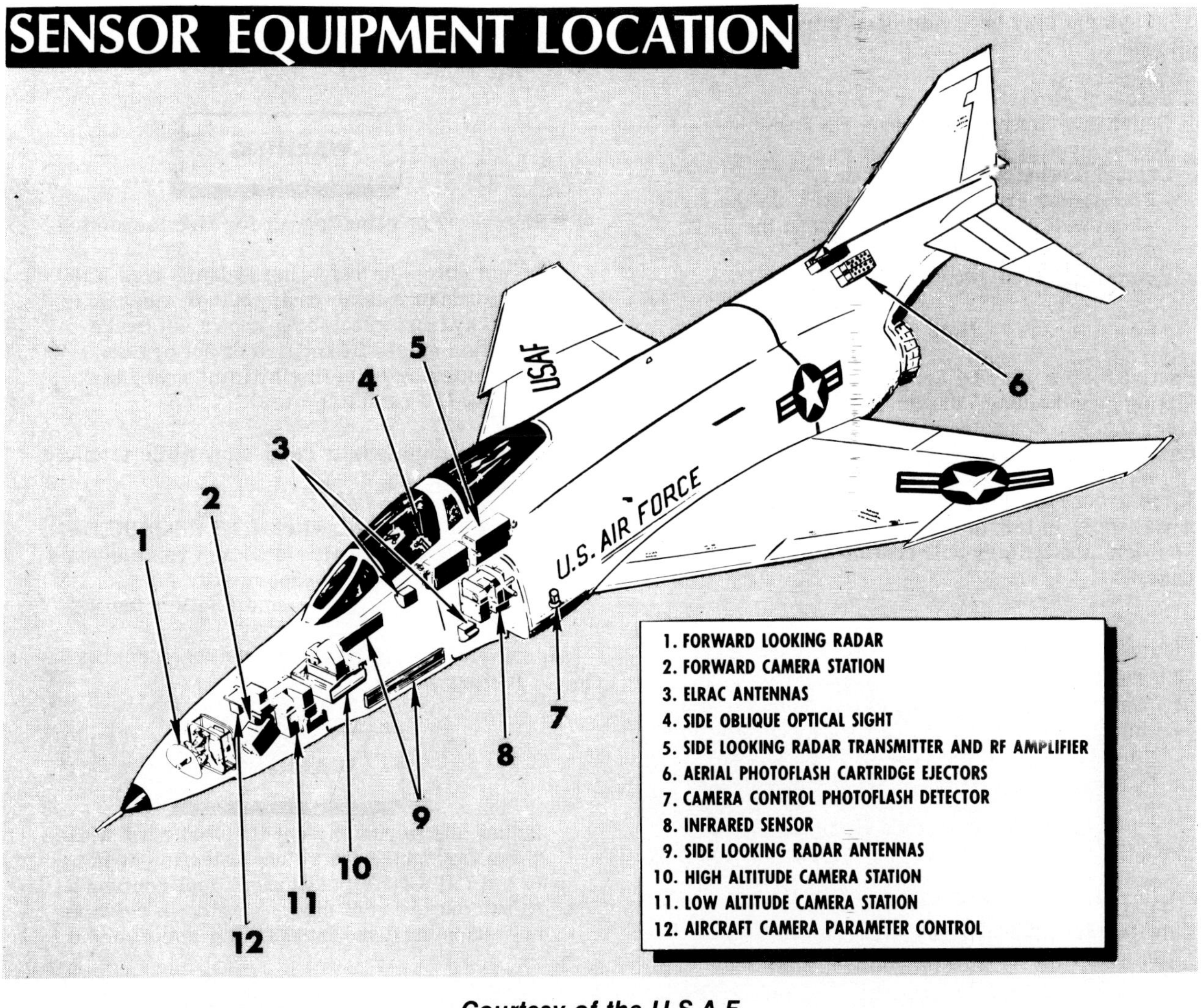

SENSOR EQUIPMENT LOCATION
USAF
U.S. AIR FORCE
1
2
3
4
5
6
7
8
9
10
11
12
1. FORWARD LOOKING RADAR
2. FORWARD CAMERA STATION
3. ELRAC ANTENNAS
4. SIDE OBLIQUE OPTICAL SIGHT
5. SIDE LOOKING RADAR TRANSMITTER AND RF AMPLIFIER
6. AERIAL PHOTOFLASH CARTRIDGE EJECTORS
7. CAMERA CONTROL PHOTOFLASH DETECTOR
8. INFRARED SENSOR
9. SIDE LOOKING RADAR ANTENNAS
10. HIGH ALTITUDE CAMERA STATION
11. LOW ALTITUDE CAMERA STATION
12. AIRCRAFT CAMERA PARAMETER CONTROL

Courtesy of the U.S.A.F.

RF-4C-23-MC, 64-1066, of the Minnesota ANG.   *(Spidle)*

RF-4C-41-MC, 69-349, of the 14th TRS at Udorn in 1973. Note the "towel rack" LORAN antenna on the spine. An ALQ-71 ECM pod is on the right inboard pylon, and an ALQ-119 pod is on the left inboard station.   *(Thurlow)*

RF-4C-37-MC, 68-555, of the 1st TRS, 10th TRW. Note the additional antennas and "bump" on the spine which are part of the ARN-101 modification.   *(France)*

RF-4C-43-MC, 69-369, at Alconbury, England on March 7, 1980. The aircraft belongs to the 1st TRS of the 10th TRW. The "A" on the tail is the remains of "AC". This was later painted "AR".   *(France)*

RF-4C
TECHNICAL DATA

Development

Letter Contract. . . . . May 62
Mock-Up . . . . Nov 62
First Flight & Delivery (YRF-4C) . . . . Aug 63
First Flight & Delivery (RF-4C) . . . . Apr 64
First Operational Delivery. . . . . Sep 64

    Optical sensors, including framing, panoramic and mapping cameras, are located in three camera stations in the nose of the aircraft. Electronic sensors include forward-looking radar, side-looking radar and an infrared reconnaissance set. Associated reconnaissance capabilities include photoflash ejection for night photography, a photographic control set, a data annotation set for recording on reconnaissance film aircraft data parameters, a HF communications set for extended communications range, a voice recorder set for recording pilot or radar observer comments, a photoflash detector, and vertical stabilized camera mounts.

C A M E R A S

	STATION	TYPE	LENS	CAMERA POSITION	MISSION
①	Forward	KS-87	6"	Fwd Oblique/Vertical	Low-Day/Night
	Forward	KS-87	3"	Fwd Oblique/Vertical	Low-Day/Night
①	Center	KA-56	3"	Vertical (Panoramic)	Low-Day
	Center	KS-87	6"3"6"	3 Camera Fan	Low-Day
	Center	KS-87	18"	Side Oblique	Hi/Low-Day
	Center	KS-87	12"	Side Oblique	Hi/Low-Day
①	Aft ②	KA-55	12"	Vertical (Panoramic)	High-Day
	Aft ②	KS-87	18"	Vertical	High-Day
	Aft	KS-87	6"	Split Vertical	Low-Day/Night
	Aft	KS-87	18"	Split Vertical	High-Day
	Aft ②	T-11	6"	Vertical (Mapping)	High-Day
	Center	KS-87	3"	Vertical	Low-Day/Night

Notes: ① Basic configuration ② Stabilized mount required

W E I G H T S

Loading	LB	L.F.
Empty	28,546 (A)	
Basic	29,741	
Design	37,500	8.5 (6.5)
Combat	*40,267	8.3 (6.3)
Max T.O.	†58,000	
Max Land	‡46,000	

(A) Actual
*   For Basic Mission
†   Limited by structure
‡   10 ft/sec design sinking speed

Note: Load factors in ( ) are for supersonic maneuvers.

F U E L

Location	Nr Tanks	Gal
Fus, bladder	6	1259
Wgs, integral	2	630
Fus, ext, drop	1	600
Wgs, ext, drop	2	740
Total		3229

Grade. JP-4
Specification MIL-J-5624

O I L

Engine, intergral . . . . 2 . .(tot) 10.3
Specification. MIL-L-7808

POWER PLANT

Nr & Model . . . .(2) J79-GE-15
Mfr. . . . . General Electric
Engine Spec Nr E-2027
Type . . . . Axial
Length with A/B . . . . 208.45 in
Diameter (max) . . . . 38.3 in
Weight (dry) . . . . .3627 lb
Tail Pipe. . . . .Variable Pos. Ejector
Augmentation . . . . .Afterburner

ENGINE RATINGS

S.L.S	LB	RPM	MIN
Max:	*17,000	7685	†30
Mil:	10,900	7685	†30
Nor:	10,300	7385	Cont

*With afterburner operating
†Below 35,000 ft, 2 hours
  Above 35,000 ft.

B O M B S

Special Weapons on Centerline Station:
MK-28 (EX or RE), MK-43 or MK-57
Practice Dispenser on Centerline Station.
SUU-21/A

ELECTRONICS

Comm-Nav Ident. AN/ASQ-88B
HF Radio. AN/ARC-105
Sound Recorder RO-254/ASQ
Navigation Computer AN/ASN-46A
AFCS AN/ASA-32J
IR Detecting Set AN/AAS-18A
Altitude-Heading Ref AN/ASN-56
Inertial Navigation AN/ASN-56
Radar Mapping Set AN/APQ-102
Radar Set AN/APQ-99
Radar Altimeter AN/APN-159
Data Display Set AN/ASQ-90
Data Recording Camera Set KS-74A
Aircraft Camera Mount Set LS-58A
Aircraft Camera Parameter Control LA-311A
Photoflash Camera Control Detector LA-285A
Countermeasures Receiving Set AN/ALR-17
Homing & Warning AN/APR-25
Warning Set AN/APR-26
ECM Pods AN/ALQ-71
                                               AN/ALQ-72
                                               AN/ALQ-87
Interference Blanker MX-7933/A

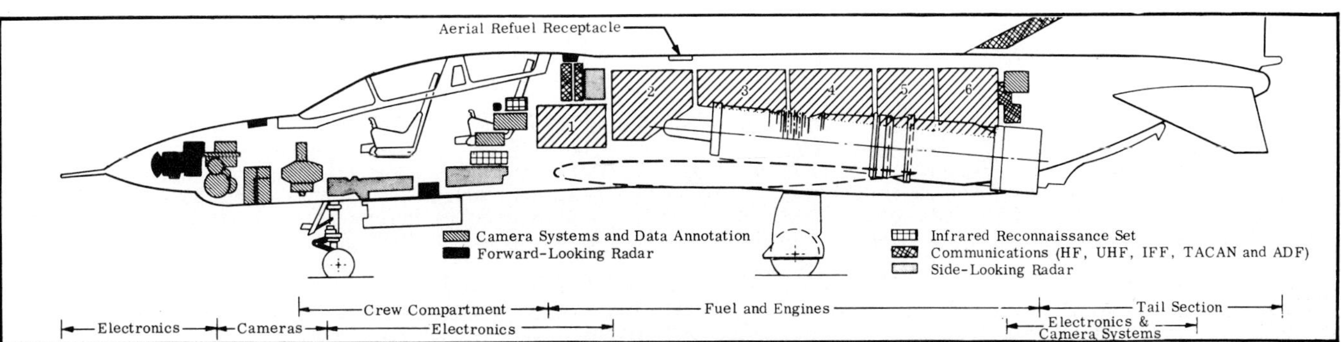

Courtesy of the U.S.A.F.

RF-4C PERFORMANCE DATA

TYPE OF MISSION		HIGH ALT. RECON	LOW ALT. RECON	NUCLEAR STRIKE	FERRY MISSION
EXTERNAL STORES LOADING		Clean + (1)600 + (2) 370 Gal. Tks.	Clean + (1)600 + (2) 370 Gal. Tks.	(1) B28 + (2) 370 Gal. Tks.	Clean + (1)600+ (2) 370 Gal. Tks.
Take-Off Gross Weight	(lb)	52,823	52,927	50,763	52,823
Fuel (JP-4 @ 6.5 lb/gal) (Int./Ext.)	(lb)	12,278/8710	12,278/8710	12,278/4810	12,278/8710
Payload - Reconnaissance Equipment	(lb)	1398	1502	1502	1398
Payload - Bombs	(lb)	None	None	2040	None
Wing Loading	(lb/sq ft)	99.7	99.9	95.8	99.7
Stall Speed (Appr. Pwr. BLC On, Wing Rock)	(kn)	148	148	145	148
Take-off Ground Run at S.L. ①	(ft)	3220	3250	2970	3220
Take-off to Clear 50 Feet ①	(ft)	3990	4000	3620	3990
Rate of Climb at S.L. ②	(fpm)	8700	8670	9500	8700
Rate of Climb at S.L. (One Engine Out) ①	(fpm)	8010	7990	8850	8010
Time: S.L. to 20,000 Ft. ② ④	(min)	3.14	3.16	2.82	3.14
Time: S.L. to 30,000 Ft. ② ④	(min)	6.02	6.05	5.34	6.02
Service Ceiling (100 FPM) ②	(ft)	34,000	33,950	35,250	34,000
Service Ceiling (One Engine Out) ①	(ft)	34,000	33,950	35,250	34,000
Combat Range ③	(n mi)	——	——	——	1418
Combat Radius ③	(n mi)	673	513	414	——
Average Speed	(kn)	499	500	499	499
Initial Cruising Altitude	(ft)	30,900	30,850	31,750	30,900
Target Speed ②	(kn)	533	635	——	——
Target Altitude	(ft)	40,050	S.L.	S.L.	——
Final Cruising Altitude	(ft)	38,800	38,750	38,850	38,800
Total Mission Time	(hr)	2.71	2.02	1.75	2.85
Combat Weight	(lb)	40,267	40,834	37,992	33,598
Combat Altitude	(ft)	40,050	S.L.	S.L.	38,200
Combat Speed ① ⑤	(kn)	1204	787	787	1207
Combat Climb ①	(fpm)	12,850	44,200	47,600	19,000
Max. Rate of Climb at S.L. ①	(fpm)	44,800	44,200	47,600	53,600
Max. Speed at 40,000 ft. ①	(kn)	1204	1203	1205	1210
Basic Speed at 35,000 ft. ① ⑤	(kn)	1196	1195	1199	1203
Landing Weight	(lb)	33,598	33,705	33,510	33,598
Ground Roll at S.L.	(ft)	3100	3110	3090	3100
Ground Roll (Parabake)	(ft)	2430	2430	2410	2430
Total from 50 ft.	(ft)	4150	4160	4140	4150
Total from 50 ft. (Parabrake)	(ft)	3490	3500	3475	3490

NOTES: ① Maximum Power ② Military Power ③ Detailed Description of Range and Radius Missions are given below. ④ Allows for Weight Reduction during Ground Operation and Climb ⑤ Installed Engine Flight Speed Limits at S.L. and 35,000 ft. are 760 and 1170 kts., respectively.

DESCRIPTION OF HIGH ALTITUDE RECON MISSION

Take-off with maximum thrust, climb on course with military thrust to optimum cruise altitude, cruise out at long range speed, climb with military thrust to cruise ceiling, conduct a 15 minute normal thrust reconnaissance run-in to target, allow 2 minutes for evasive action at normal thrust, conduct an 8 minute escape with normal thrust, cruise back to base at cruise altitude at long range speed. Range free allowances include 5 minutes at normal thrust and 1 minute at max thrust at sea level static for starting engines and take-off, 2 minutes of evasive action at normal thrust at combat altitude and a reserve of 20 minutes loiter at sea level at speeds for maximum endurance (two engines) plus 5% of initial fuel load.

DESCRIPTION OF LOW ALTITUDE RECON MISSION

Take-off with maximum thrust, climb on course with military thrust to optimum cruise altitude, cruise out at long range speed, descend to sea level (no credit for fuel or distance), conduct a 50 nautical mile reconnaissance run-in to target at military thrust and a 50 nautical mile run-out at military thrust, climb on course with military thrust to optimum cruise altitude, cruise back to base at long range speed. Range free allowances include 5 minutes at normal thrust and 1 minute at max thrust at sea level static for starting engines and take-off and a reserve of 20 minutes loiter at sea level at speeds for maximum endurance (two engines) plus 5% of initial fuel load.

DESCRIPTION OF NUCLEAR STRIKE MISSION

Take-off with maximum thrust, climb on course with military thrust to optimum cruise altitude, cruise out at long range speed, descend to sea level (no credit for fuel or distance), search out target for 5 minutes at 0.8 Mach at sea level, expend store, climb on course with military thrust to optimum cruise altitude, cruise back to base at long range speed. Range free allowances include 5 minutes at normal thrust and 1 minute at max thrust at sea level static for starting engines and take-off, 5 minute search at sea level and a reserve of 20 minutes loiter at sea level at speeds for maximum endurance (two engines) plus 5% of initial fuel load.

DESCRIPTION OF FERRY MISSION

Take-off with maximum thrust, climb on course with military thrust to optimum cruise altitude, cruise out at long range speeds to remote base. Range free allowances include 5 minutes at normal thrust and 1 minute at maximum thrust at sea level static for starting engines and take-off, and a reserve of 20 minutes loiter at sea level at speeds for maximum endurance (two engines) plus 5% of initial fuel load.

Data and Information courtesy of the U.S. Air Force.

RF-4C EXTERIOR ORIENTATION

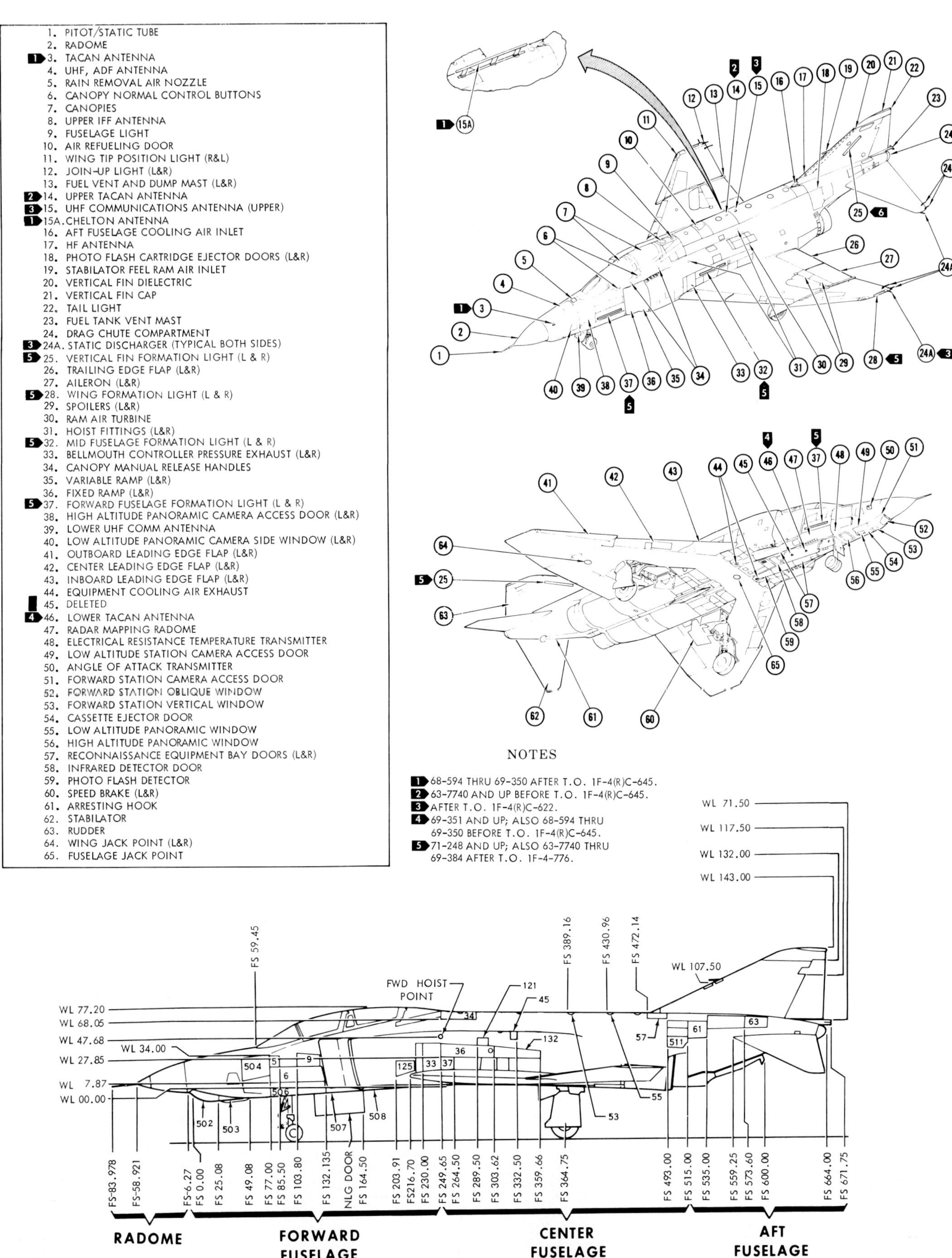

Courtesy of the U.S.A.F.

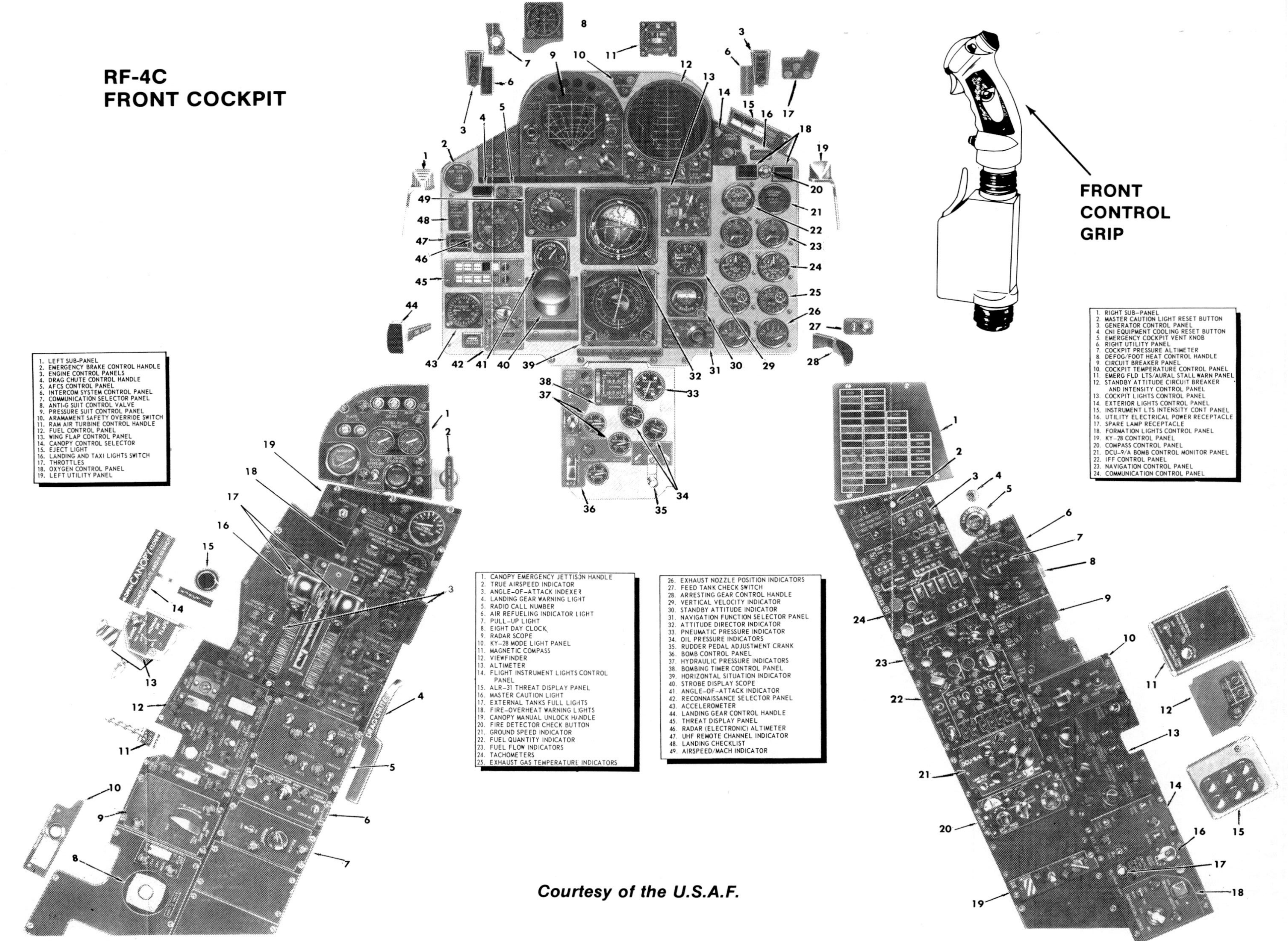

RF-4C
FRONT COCKPIT

FRONT CONTROL GRIP

Courtesy of the U.S.A.F.

1. RIGHT SUB-PANEL
2. MASTER CAUTION LIGHT RESET BUTTON
3. GENERATOR CONTROL PANEL
4. CNI EQUIPMENT COOLING RESET BUTTON
5. EMERGENCY COCKPIT VENT KNOB
6. RIGHT UTILITY PANEL
7. COCKPIT PRESSURE ALTIMETER
8. DEFOG/FOOT HEAT CONTROL HANDLE
9. CIRCUIT BREAKER PANEL
10. COCKPIT TEMPERATURE CONTROL PANEL
11. EMERG FLD LTS/AURAL STALL WARN PANEL
12. STANDBY ATTITUDE CIRCUIT BREAKER
    AND INTENSITY CONTROL PANEL
13. COCKPIT LIGHTS CONTROL PANEL
14. EXTERIOR LIGHTS CONTROL PANEL
15. INSTRUMENT LTS INTENSITY CONT PANEL
16. UTILITY ELECTRICAL POWER RECEPTACLE
17. SPARE LAMP RECEPTACLE
18. FORMATION LIGHTS CONTROL PANEL
19. KY-28 CONTROL PANEL
20. COMPASS CONTROL PANEL
21. DCU-9/A BOMB CONTROL MONITOR PANEL
22. IFF CONTROL PANEL
23. NAVIGATION CONTROL PANEL
24. COMMUNICATION CONTROL PANEL

1. CANOPY EMERGENCY JETTISON HANDLE
2. TRUE AIRSPEED INDICATOR
3. ANGLE-OF-ATTACK INDEXER
4. LANDING GEAR WARNING LIGHT
5. RADIO CALL NUMBER
6. AIR REFUELING INDICATOR LIGHT
7. PULL-UP LIGHT
8. EIGHT DAY CLOCK
9. RADAR SCOPE
10. KY-28 MODE LIGHT PANEL
11. MAGNETIC COMPASS
12. VIEWFINDER
13. ALTIMETER
14. FLIGHT INSTRUMENT LIGHTS CONTROL
    PANEL
15. ALR-31 THREAT DISPLAY PANEL
16. MASTER CAUTION LIGHT
17. EXTERNAL TANKS FULL LIGHTS
18. FIRE-OVERHEAT WARNING LIGHTS
19. CANOPY MANUAL UNLOCK HANDLE
20. FIRE DETECTOR CHECK BUTTON
21. GROUND SPEED INDICATOR
22. FUEL QUANTITY INDICATOR
23. FUEL FLOW INDICATORS
24. TACHOMETERS
25. EXHAUST GAS TEMPERATURE INDICATORS

26. EXHAUST NOZZLE POSITION INDICATORS
27. FEED TANK CHECK SWITCH
28. ARRESTING GEAR CONTROL HANDLE
29. VERTICAL VELOCITY INDICATOR
30. STANDBY ATTITUDE INDICATOR
31. NAVIGATION FUNCTION SELECTOR PANEL
32. ATTITUDE DIRECTOR INDICATOR
33. PNEUMATIC PRESSURE INDICATOR
34. OIL PRESSURE INDICATORS
35. RUDDER PEDAL ADJUSTMENT CRANK
36. BOMB CONTROL PANEL
37. HYDRAULIC PRESSURE INDICATORS
38. BOMBING TIMER CONTROL PANEL
39. HORIZONTAL SITUATION INDICATOR
40. STROBE DISPLAY SCOPE
41. ANGLE-OF-ATTACK INDICATOR
42. RECONNAISSANCE SELECTOR PANEL
43. ACCELEROMETER
44. LANDING GEAR CONTROL HANDLE
45. THREAT DISPLAY PANEL
46. RADAR (ELECTRONIC) ALTIMETER
47. UHF REMOTE CHANNEL INDICATOR
48. LANDING CHECKLIST
49. AIRSPEED/MACH INDICATOR

1. LEFT SUB-PANEL
2. EMERGENCY BRAKE CONTROL HANDLE
3. ENGINE CONTROL PANELS
4. DRAG CHUTE CONTROL HANDLE
5. AFCS CONTROL PANEL
6. INTERCOM SYSTEM CONTROL PANEL
7. COMMUNICATION SELECTOR PANEL
8. ANTI-G SUIT CONTROL VALVE
9. PRESSURE SUIT CONTROL PANEL
10. ARAMAMENT SAFETY OVERRIDE SWITCH
11. RAM AIR TURBINE CONTROL HANDLE
12. FUEL CONTROL PANEL
13. WING FLAP CONTROL PANEL
14. CANOPY CONTROL SELECTOR
15. EJECT LIGHT
16. LANDING AND TAXI LIGHTS SWITCH
17. THROTTLES
18. OXYGEN CONTROL PANEL
19. LEFT UTILITY PANEL

RF-4C
REAR COCKPIT

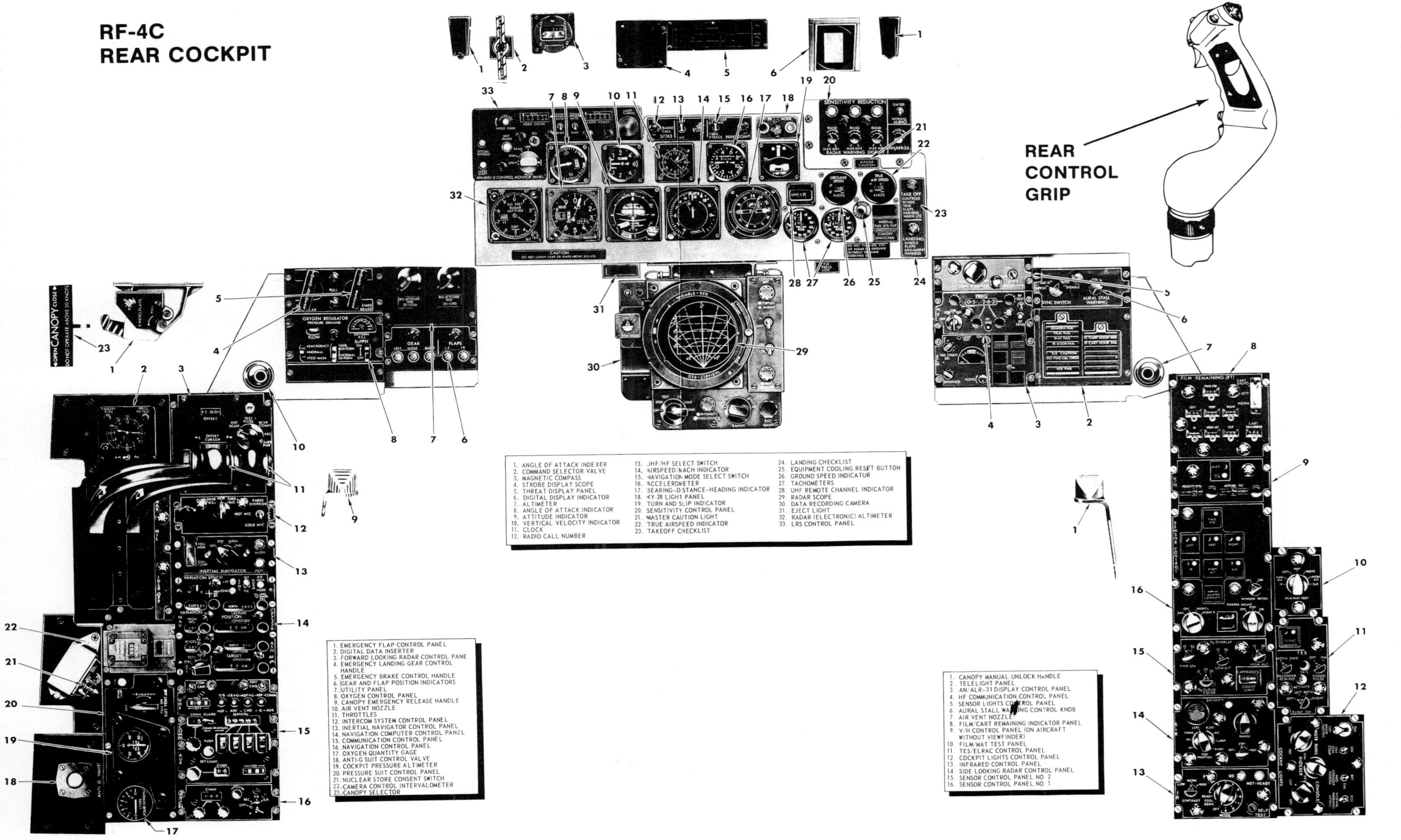

REAR
CONTROL
GRIP

1. ANGLE OF ATTACK INDEXER
2. COMMAND SELECTOR VALVE
3. MAGNETIC COMPASS
4. STROBE DISPLAY SCOPE
5. THREAT DISPLAY PANEL
6. DIGITAL DISPLAY INDICATOR
7. ALTIMETER
8. ANGLE OF ATTACK INDICATOR
9. ATTITUDE INDICATOR
10. VERTICAL VELOCITY INDICATOR
11. CLOCK
12. RADIO CALL NUMBER
13. JHF/HF SELECT SWITCH
14. AIRSPEED/MACH INDICATOR
15. NAVIGATION MODE SELECT SWITCH
16. BEARING-DISTANCE-HEADING INDICATOR
17. ACCELEROMETER
18. KY-28 LIGHT PANEL
19. TURN AND SLIP INDICATOR
20. SENSITIVITY CONTROL PANEL
21. MASTER CAUTION LIGHT
22. TRUE AIRSPEED INDICATOR
23. TAKEOFF CHECKLIST
24. LANDING CHECKLIST
25. EQUIPMENT COOLING RESET BUTTON
26. GROUND SPEED INDICATOR
27. TACHOMETERS
28. UHF REMOTE CHANNEL INDICATOR
29. RADAR SCOPE
30. DATA RECORDING CAMERA
31. EJECT LIGHT
32. RADAR (ELECTRONIC) ALTIMETER
33. LRS CONTROL PANEL

1. EMERGENCY FLAP CONTROL PANEL
2. DIGITAL DATA INSERTER
3. FORWARD LOOKING RADAR CONTROL PANE
4. EMERGENCY LANDING GEAR CONTROL HANDLE
5. EMERGENCY BRAKE CONTROL HANDLE
6. GEAR AND FLAP POSITION INDICATORS
7. UTILITY PANEL
8. OXYGEN CONTROL PANEL
9. CANOPY EMERGENCY RELEASE HANDLE
10. AIR VENT NOZZLE
11. THROTTLES
12. INTERCOM SYSTEM CONTROL PANEL
13. INERTIAL NAVIGATOR CONTROL PANEL
14. NAVIGATION COMPUTER CONTROL PANEL
15. COMMUNICATION CONTROL PANEL
16. NAVIGATION CONTROL PANEL
17. OXYGEN QUANTITY GAGE
18. ANTI-G SUIT CONTROL VALVE
19. COCKPIT PRESSURE ALTIMETER
20. PRESSURE SUIT CONTROL PANEL
21. NUCLEAR STORE CONSENT SWITCH
22. CAMERA CONTROL INTERVALOMETER
23. CANOPY SELECTOR

1. CANOPY MANUAL UNLOCK HANDLE
2. TELELIGHT PANEL
3. AN/ALR-31 DISPLAY CONTROL PANEL
4. HF COMMUNICATION CONTROL PANEL
5. SENSOR LIGHTS CONTROL PANEL
6. AURAL STALL WARNING CONTROL KNOB
7. AIR VENT NOZZLE
8. FILM/CART REMAINING INDICATOR PANEL
9. V/H CONTROL PANEL (ON AIRCRAFT WITHOUT VIEWFINDER)
10. FILM/MAT TEST PANEL
11. TES/ELRAC CONTROL PANEL
12. COCKPIT LIGHTS CONTROL PANEL
13. INFRARED CONTROL PANEL
14. SIDE LOOKING RADAR CONTROL PANEL
15. SENSOR CONTROL PANEL NO 2
16. SENSOR CONTROL PANEL NO 1

Courtesy of the U.S.A.F.

RF-4C DETAILS

Close-up of the nose on an all white RF-4C. Note the yaw string hanging to the side over the anti-glare panel.
(McDonnell-Douglas)

There have been two noses used on the RF-4C as shown by these two photos. The nose on the left was the first one used, and was relatively straight underneath. The nose on the right is the newer nose, and is more rounded underneath. Both versions are still in use.

The RF-4C has no Sparrow missile bays. The area where the two rear bays would normally be is flush with the underside of the fuselage. However, there are fairings where the forward missile bays would be as shown in this photo. These fairings reduce drag and smooth the airflow under the aircraft.

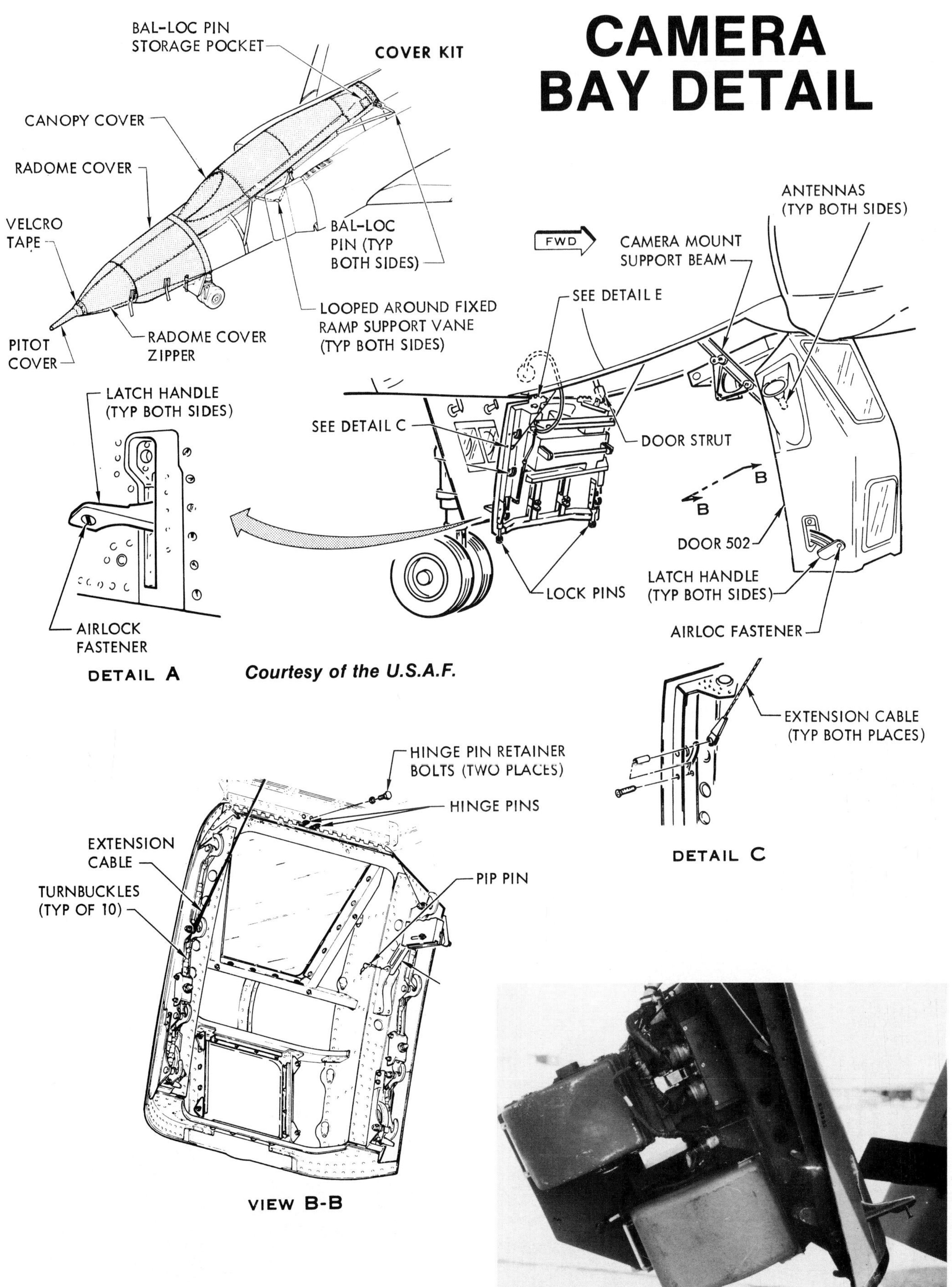

CAMERA BAY DETAIL

Courtesy of the U.S.A.F.

Left side view of the rear camera bay door in the open position with the camera in place.   (Leader)

Forward-looking, still picture camera in an RF-4C.
(Leader)

Downward-looking, still picture camera on open door.
(Leader)

AN/APQ-99 RADAR

RF-4C radar pulled out and turned to the right for access to electronic chassis.
(Leader)

RF-4C radar in position with antenna looking forward.
(Leader)

PHOTO RECON EQUIPMENT LOCATIONS

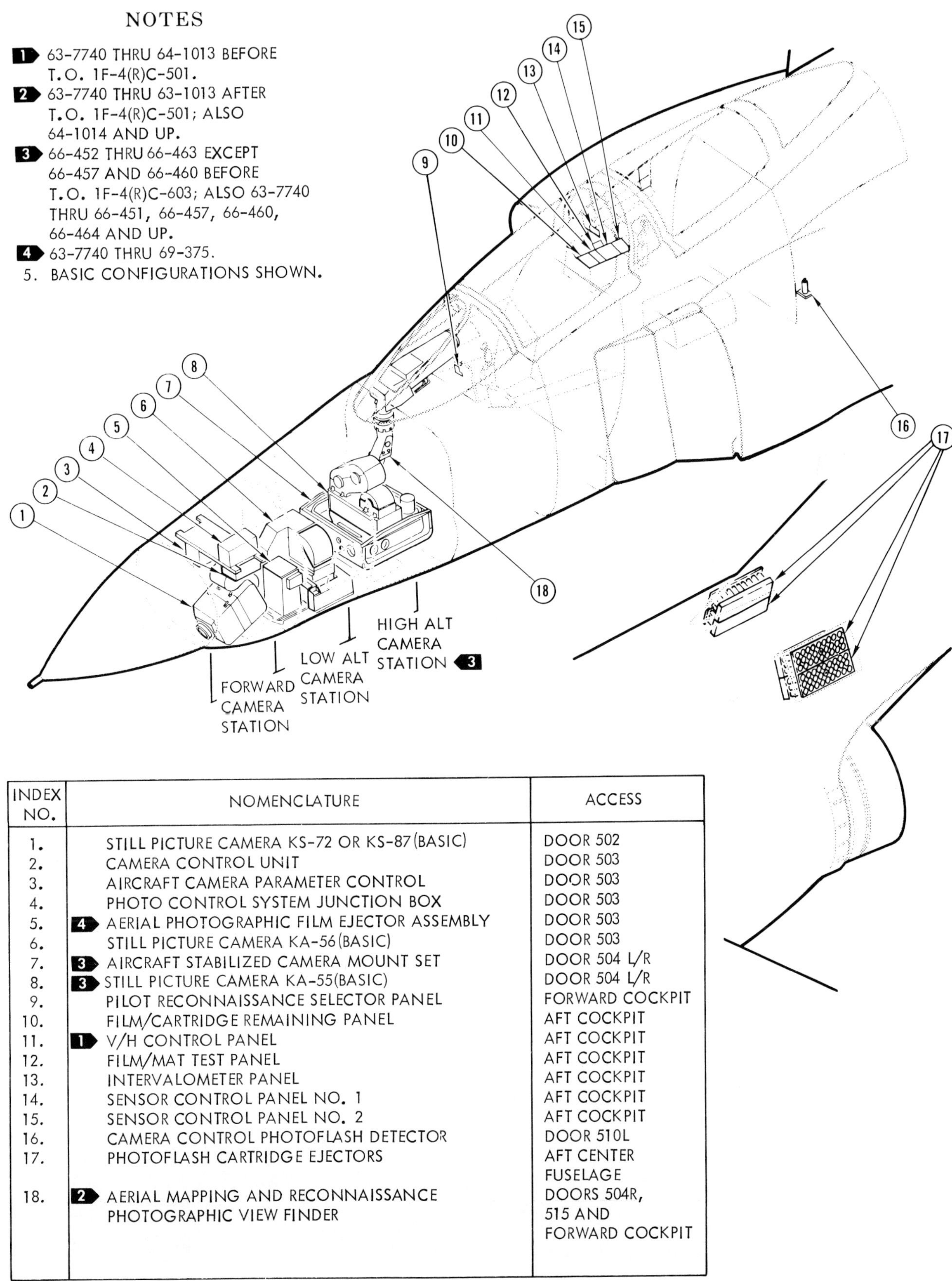

INDEX NO.	NOMENCLATURE	ACCESS
1.	STILL PICTURE CAMERA KS-72 OR KS-87 (BASIC)	DOOR 502
2.	CAMERA CONTROL UNIT	DOOR 503
3.	AIRCRAFT CAMERA PARAMETER CONTROL	DOOR 503
4.	PHOTO CONTROL SYSTEM JUNCTION BOX	DOOR 503
5.	4 AERIAL PHOTOGRAPHIC FILM EJECTOR ASSEMBLY	DOOR 503
6.	STILL PICTURE CAMERA KA-56 (BASIC)	DOOR 503
7.	3 AIRCRAFT STABILIZED CAMERA MOUNT SET	DOOR 504 L/R
8.	3 STILL PICTURE CAMERA KA-55 (BASIC)	DOOR 504 L/R
9.	PILOT RECONNAISSANCE SELECTOR PANEL	FORWARD COCKPIT
10.	FILM/CARTRIDGE REMAINING PANEL	AFT COCKPIT
11.	1 V/H CONTROL PANEL	AFT COCKPIT
12.	FILM/MAT TEST PANEL	AFT COCKPIT
13.	INTERVALOMETER PANEL	AFT COCKPIT
14.	SENSOR CONTROL PANEL NO. 1	AFT COCKPIT
15.	SENSOR CONTROL PANEL NO. 2	AFT COCKPIT
16.	CAMERA CONTROL PHOTOFLASH DETECTOR	DOOR 510L
17.	PHOTOFLASH CARTRIDGE EJECTORS	AFT CENTER FUSELAGE
18.	2 AERIAL MAPPING AND RECONNAISSANCE PHOTOGRAPHIC VIEW FINDER	DOORS 504R, 515 AND FORWARD COCKPIT

Courtesy of the U.S.A.F.

STORE	NOTES	STATION LOADING					CARRIAGE						JETTISON		
							AIRSPEED		ACCEL G		ROLL RATE DEG/SEC	STICK THROW	MIN	MAX	
		1	2	3	4	5	KIAS	MACH	SYM.	UNSYM			KIAS	KIAS	M
McDonnell 600 Gallon CL Tank	See Notes 1 and 2.	Empty to 10% Full * (station 3)					(airplane symbol)	(airplane symbol)	(airplane symbol) (Upper) −2.0 (Lower)	(airplane symbol)	200	FULL	Below 35,000 feet NE | 375 | NE Above 35,000 feet NE | 420 | NE		
		10% Full To 75% Full (station 3)					(airplane symbol)	(airplane symbol)	+ 6.5 −2.0	+ 5.2 0.0	150	1/2	Not Authorized		
		75% Full To Full * (station 3)					(airplane symbol)	(airplane symbol)	+ 5.0 −2.0	+ 4.0 0.0	150	1/2	Below 35,000 feet NE | 375 | NE Above 35,000 feet NE | 420 | NE		
Royal Jet 600 Gallon CL Tank	See Notes 1 and 3.	Empty to 10% Full * (station 3)					600	1.8	+ 5.0 0.0	+ 4.0 + 1.0	**	**	Below 35,000 feet NE | 375 | NE Above 35,000 feet NE | 420 | NE		
		10% Full To 75% Full (station 3)					600	1.8	+ 5.0 0.0	+ 4.0 + 1.0	**	**	Not Authorized		
		75% Full To Full * (station 3)					600	1.8	+ 3.0 0.0	+ 1.0 + 1.0	**	**	Below 35,000 feet NE | 375 | NE Above 35,000 feet NE | 420 | NE		
McDonnell 370 Gallon Wing Tank and Sergeant Fletcher 370 Gallon Wing Tank	See Notes 2, 5, and 12.	(station 1)	Empty to 10% Full *			(station 5)	750	1.6	+ 6.0 −2.0	+ 4.8 0.0	270	Full	BELOW 35,000 FT: (1G Level Flight) 175 to 375, (2G Sym Flight) 400 to 445, (3G Sym Flight) 425 to 510. ABOVE 35,000 FT: (1G Level Flight) 175 to 410, (2G Sym Flight) 440 to 490, (3G Sym Flight) 460 to 550.		
		(station 1)	10% Full to 75% Full			(station 5)	550	1.6	+ 5.0 −2.0	+ 4.0 0.0	120	1/2			
		(station 1)	75% Full to Full *			(station 5)	550	1.6	+ 4.0 −1.0	+ 2.0 0.0	120	1/2			
SUU–21/A Dispenser	See Notes 2 and 4.			(station 3)			550	1.3	+ 6.5 −3.0	+ 5.2 0.0	150	Full	Not Jettisonable		
B28 Bomb, B43 Bomb, B57 Bomb or Dummy Unit	See Notes 2 and 6.			(station 3)			(airplane symbol)	(airplane symbol)	+ 6.5 −3.0	+ 5.2 0.0	150	Full	NE	(airplane symbol)	(airplane symbol)

Fuel tank dollies with two 370 gallon wing tanks and one 600 gallon centerline tank. Except for ECM pods, fuel tanks are about the only external store usually seen on an RF-4C.

(Thurlow)

STORE	NOTES	STATION LOADING					CARRIAGE				ROLL RATE DEG/SEC	STICK THROW	JETTISON		
		1	2	3	4	5	AIRSPEED		ACCEL G				MIN	MAX	
							KIAS	MACH	SYM.	UNSYM			KIAS	KIAS	M
ALQ–71/QRC–160A–1. ALQ–72/QRC–160A–2. ALQ–87/QRC–160A–8. ECM PODS.	See Notes 1, 2, and 7. (with RAT)		⬤		⬤		✈	✈	+6.0 −3.0	+4.8 0.0	200	FULL	Below 25,000 feet 385 Single Speed Above 25,000 feet 410	Below 25,000 feet 385 Single Speed Above 25,000 feet 410	NE 1.1
ALQ–71/QRC–160A–1. ALQ–72/QRC–160A–2. ALQ–87/QRC–160A–8. ECM PODS.	See Notes 1, 2, 7, 8, and 9. (with or without RAT)		⬤		⬤		✈	✈	+6.0 −3.0	+4.8 0.0	200	FULL			
ALQ–71/QRC–160A–1. ALQ–72/QRC–160A–2. ALQ–87/QRC–160A–8. ALQ–101. ALQ–71(V)–3. QRC–335A(V)–3. QRC–335A(V)–4.	See Notes 1, 2, 10, 11. (without RAT)		⬤		⬤		✈	✈	+6.0 −3.0	+4.8 0.0	✈	FULL			

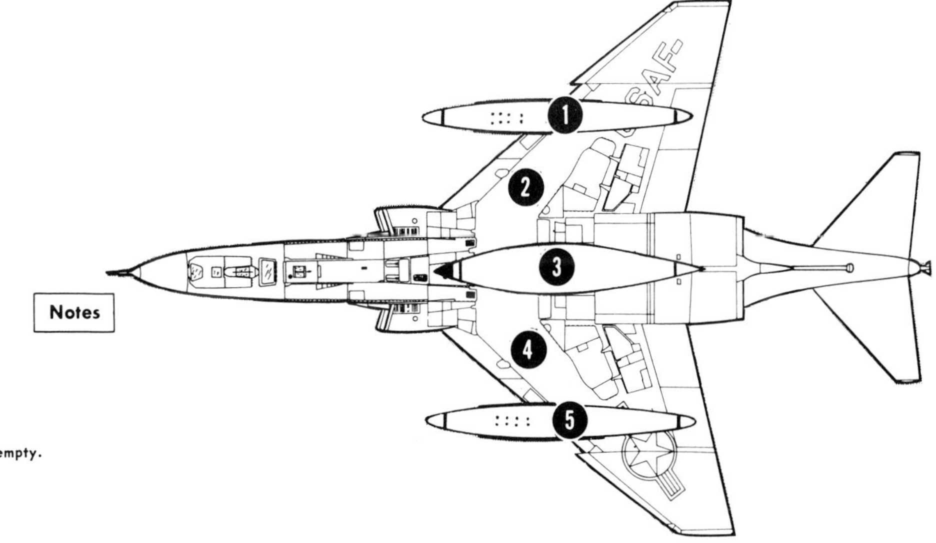

Notes

✈ Aircraft limits

NE = Not Established

NA = Not Applicable

✱ External tanks must be jettisoned either full or empty.

✱✱ Only gradual coordinated turns are permitted.

1. Jettison 1G level flight.

2. If gross weight is over 37,500 lbs., refer to Acceleration Limitations Chart.

3. If gross weight is over 45,000 lbs., refer to Acceleration Limitations Chart.

4. Employment limit same as Carriage limit.

5. All tanks must be pressurized in the normal manner.

6. Releasing and jettisoning special weapons are based on special considerations. Refer to T.O. 1F–4C–25 series publications to obtain jettison/release criteria and additional limitations as imposed by the weapon. Maximum release speed same as aircraft limits.

7. Carriage speed may be reduced by ECM pod ram air turbine temperature limits.

8. After T.O. 1F–4(R)C–604 and 605. ECM pods may be carried with or without ram air turbine.

9. Roll Rate for ECM pods without ram air turbine is the basic aircraft limits.

10. After T.O. 1F–4(R)C–626 and 627. ECM pods will not have ram air turbines.

11. QRC–335A(V)–3 and –4 pod: jettison single speed is 500 KIAS. Jettison must be accomplished with 0 ejection force.

12. Jettison not authorized when tanks are 10% Full to 75% Full. External tanks must be jettisoned either full or empty.

Courtesy of the U.S.A.F.

MODELER'S SECTION

KIT REVIEWS

F-4C & F-4D KITS

Lindberg 1/100th Scale F-4D

We simply cannot recommend this kit for the serious scale modeler. Its shape, proportions, and dimensions are all incorrect right down to the Sparrow missiles which are way too fat. The best that could be said is that this kit is a "representation" of the Phantom, and is not a scale model - but even that is stretching it a bit. Enough said!

Revell 1/72nd Scale F-4C/D

This kit was one of the first released on the Phantom, and in its original form was a Navy F-4B. Revell re-released it in their "Air Commando" series as a USAF F-4C, but in truth it still represents the F-4B. Most noticeable is that the kit has the thin wings of the F-4B and not the thicker wings and main landing gear characteristic of the F-4C or -D. The cockpit is very sparse, and has only vertical pieces of plastic molded into the cockpit interior to represent seats. There are no control columns except for a representation that is molded on the pilot figures.

The general outline is fairly good for an F-4B, and considering its age, the kit is not too bad. Decals for the "Air Commando" release are very basic consisting of national insignia, a tail number with "USAF" above it, a red warning stripe, and a couple of other basics. External stores consist only of four Sparrow missiles and two external fuel tanks on the outboard wing pylons. No inboard or centerline pylons are provided. Wheel wells are open and contain no detail. A flat piece of plastic extends across the forward end of the nose gear well, and the nose strut attaches to it rather than extending up into the well.

The kit has been released several times with modifications to an F-4J, F-4K, and with even a more extensive rework to an F-4E. As later released in a Blue Angels set of four F-4J's, Revell made an attempt at adding the wing bulges and a RHAW

Revell 1/72nd F-4C with external stores added from other kits. This model does not build up into an accurate F-4C or F-4D since it does not have the bulges on the wings or the thicker tires.

antenna to the top of the tail. However these two modifications leave something to be desired, which is unfortunate. Had they been done properly, these modifications would have allowed the modeler to make a few other easy changes (add an IR sensor under the nose and use the shorter afterburner cans from an earlier release of the same kit), and the result would be a more accurate F-4C or -D.

Even considering these faults, for a modeler who wants to build a 1/72nd F-4C or F-4D straight out of the box, this is the best kit to use. The only competition in this scale is the Airfix model, (reviewed next) and it has all the problems of the Revell kit and a few more.

Airfix 1/72nd Scale F-4

This is the oldest Phantom kit available in this scale, with the first issue appearing some 17 or 18 years ago. It was originally issued as an F-4B (non-bulged wing and no slatted stab) and as the Phantom itself evolved, so did this kit. In its most current release, parts are included to build B, C, D, E, and J variants. However, the wing and stabilators remain as per the original offering.

The kit has sparse, mostly incorrect surface detail. Cockpit consists of two figures, two seats, forward control stick and floorboard, all of dubious value. Landing gear is fair with two sets of main gear wheels provided. Stores include three drop tanks, six Sparrow missiles, a couple of Navy-style inboard station pylons with TERs molded integral and six 750 lb. bombs plus two underwing gunpods. Scalewise the model is not too bad, both dimensions and proportions being generally correct. Both noses provided need much reworking to give the proper appearance. The glass is in three pieces and will require much reworking. Decals by Scalemaster provide markings for the 388th TFW in the latest release of this kit by US/Airfix. (Washington D.C. IPMS/USA).

Building a Better F-4C or D in 1/72nd Scale

Surprisingly enough, there is no kit of the F-4 in 1/72nd scale that accurately represents the F-4C or F-4D version. The biggest problem is that none of the kits has the proper wing bulges and wider landing gear that is characteristic of these two versions as well as the later F-4E and F-4J. However, it is possible to build an accurate -C or -D by using the following procedure. Buy a Hasegawa/Minicraft F-4E (one of the older ones that does not have the leading edge slats), and also get a Revell F-4B or an Airfix kit in 1/72nd scale. We recommend the Revell kit because the nose is too blunt on the Airfix model. The Hasegawa/Minicraft F-4E will form the basis for the conversion since it is the only F-4 model in 1/72nd scale that correctly represents the wing bulges and wider landing gear. Cut the longer F-4E nose off of the Hasegawa model on the vertical panel line just in front of the windscreen and even with the forward wall of the nose landing gear well. Next, cut off the nose of the Revell kit (or Airfix) in the same place, and attach it to the Hasegawa fuselage. Use the nose landing gear strut from the Hasegawa kit, but replace the nose gear doors with those from the Revell or Airfix kit. The IR sensor should also be added under the nose, but may have to be modified some in the case of the F-4D.

The Hasegawa kit has the longer afterburner cans, and these should be replaced with the shorter ones from the Revell or Airfix kit. If the Airfix kit is used, both the long and short cans are supplied, so be sure to use the short ones. The Hasegawa kit also has the horizontal stabilizers with the leading edge slot, so this must be replaced with non-slotted stabilizers from the Revell or Airfix kit. If the Airfix stabs are used they will require more plastic surgery than those from the Revell kit where they join the fuselage. The F-4C & D also had a second pitot tube on the vertical stabilizer, so this must be added from sprue or a pin. See the drawings in this book for the proper location of these tubes. Lastly, by adding the appropriate small antennas on the spine and forward nose landing gear door, an excellent model of the F-4C or F-4D will result, and it will be considerably more accurate than any available kit built from stock.

By using the Airtec or Airmodel RF-4 noses, the same procedure can be used to build an RF-4C. However the Sparrow missile bays will also have to be filled in since they are not present on the RF-4 version.

While these conversions are relatively simple, it would be nice if one of the model companies would develop a good 1/72nd scale kit of the F-4C and -D and another one for the RF-4C. The main problem with the existing kits is that they are old and show their age. Additionally, manufacturers have tried to represent too many versions of the Phantom with too few changes to their kits. It would seem that this classic aircraft deserves far better representation in the most popular of all modeling scales.

F-4C built using the Hasegawa F-4E kit, and a nose from an Airfix F-4 kit as described in the narrative.

Monogram 1/48th Scale F-4C/D

Detail & Scale recommends this kit as the best available of the Phantom in any scale. Monogram obviously did extensive research for the development of this kit, and it shows in the accuracy and details of the finished product.

The kit has many extras such as two different

ECM pods, a camera pod, and the "towel rack" antenna for the spine of the aircraft. Also included is a small "bump" to be added to the nose IR sensor if the builder chooses to build the -D version. Armament is limited to the air-to-air variety, consisting of four Sidewinders and four Sparrow missiles. Supplementing these is a Vulcan cannon pod for the centerline pylon. Fuel tanks are provided for the outboard pylons, but the option for a centerline 600 gallon tank is not provided. It would have been nice if some air-to-ground ordnance had been provided, but a variety of such ordnance is available from other Monogram 1/48th scale kits, so it can be obtained if the modeler is willing to bear the extra expense.

Fit of the kit is quite good with two exceptions. The gap where the horizontal stabilizers join the fuselage is quite excessive, and will require some filling and sanding. Second, the instrument panel in the front cockpit is not "tall" enough in that there is a gap between the top of the panel and the fuselage. Some adjustments in the mounting of the instrument panel are required to raise it high enough to eliminate this gap.

The rest of the cockpit is excellent, and the seats are the best in any F-4 model. Ejection seat handles are missing on the right side and center of the seats, but these are easily added. The rest of the seat is a gem with good representation of the head rests, seat belts, face curtain rings, and parachute pack on top. Consoles are molded into the plastic rather than being decals, and this is the way it should be in a kit in 1/48th scale. Instrument panels have the instruments molded on them which gives a good 3-dimensional effect to the panel rather than the flat effect of a decal. Even the circuit breaker panels and other details are molded into the fuselage sides inside the cockpit.

Scribing on the model is of the raised type, and is very delicate and accurate. We had to look very hard to find any errors, but we did find that two connectors on the inboard pylons, and the panel lines on the outboard pylons were incorrect. This is not intended to be as much a criticism as it is an example of how hard it is to find something wrong with this kit.

Decals are provided for three aircraft. One, flown by Col. Robin Olds, and another flown by Steve Ritchie are quite well known. The fact that both of these pilots were "MiG killers" probably explains the choice of air-to-air ordnance supplied in the kit. The third Phantom represented on the decal sheet is an F-4D from the 23rd TFS, 52nd TFW at Spangdahlem Air Base, Germany in 1976. It too has MiG-kill stars on its splitter plates.

The decals include all major markings and a considerable amount of the smaller stenciling. Monogram's decals do not seem to adhere very well to even a gloss finish, and decal silvering will result unless care is taken to insure that the decal film is making a good seal on the model.

The landing gear is well done, and the gear wells are nicely detailed. The speed brakes are separate pieces and can be placed in the open position. However, the activating cylinder is molded into the well, and once the speed brakes are attached there is a noticeable gap between the oleo part of the cylinder and the speed brake itself. But the fact that the speed brake is open is a step ahead of other kits since it is normal for it to be in the open position when the aircraft is on the ground.

Overall, we highly recommend this kit as the best available of the Phantom.

Review sample courtesy of Monogram

<u>UPC thru Entex 1/48th Scale F-4</u>

This kit has appeared in the logo of several different manufacturers with Entex the current distributor (musical molds!). It has little to recommend it since it was a poor offering when originally issued by UPC some fifteen years ago. The model is designed with working features such as retractable landing gear, fully movable control surfaces, removable engines, etc. None of it works as advertised, and on the whole it is advisable to pass on this one especially by virtue of its retail price (high). Accuracy is something that was overlooked when the molds were cut, fit is poor, and detailing incorrect throughout. Internal fuel tanks are no longer visible once the model is assembled, and one wonders what the designer had in mind when he included them. The model, in a

Monogram 1/48th scale F-4C/D kit. This is the best F-4 kit on the market.

word, is crude. We simply cannot recommend it with the better kits that are now available in 1/48th scale.

<u>ESCI, Scalecraft 1/48th Scale F-4C/D</u>

This kit is quite an improvement over some of this company's earlier releases. While not as good as the Monogram kit, this model has a lot to recommend it. It is properly scaled and proportioned, and molded in olive drab. Quality of the clear parts is exceptional, landing gear, wells, and doors are well-detailed.

About the same time this kit was released, ESCI also released the kit as an F-4E. Unfortunately they did not make all of the changes needed between the two versions. This -C/-D version has the same slotted stabilizers as the -E kit. These slots are very poorly done, and do not even belong on the -C or -D. Additionally, there is no IR sensor provided for the F-4D. Only the -C type sensor is provided.

The decals are quite well done with good colors and excellent registration. The one bad spot is the decals for the instument panels. These do not even remotely resemble the instrument panels on any version of the Phantom. The kit pieces that these decals go on are likewise incorrect, and are best discarded. Decals are provided for an F-4C wing commander's aircraft of the 58th TFW at Luke AFB, an F-4D of the 4th TFW at Seymour Johnson AFB, and a Spanish C-12 at Torrejon AB.

Ordnance is limited to the air-to-air variety, with Sidewinders and Sparrows provided. Two 370 gallon wing tanks and a 600 gallon centerline tank are included, and the 600 gallon tank is particularly welcome since it is missing in the Monogram and Revell 1/48th scale Phantoms.

Overall this kit is not quite as good as the Monogram kit, but it is very worthwhile, and may be the best kit that this company has produced. We recommend this kit.

Review sample courtesy of Scalecraft

RF-4C KITS
<u>IMC 1/72nd Scale RF-4</u>

Released in the "Battle Damage" series, this kit is an obvious modification of the Revell mold. The earlier style recon nose replaces the standard nose, and the Sparrow missile bays have been filled in. However, the forward bays are merely covered over even with the fuselage rather than having the fairings which are present on the actual aircraft.

The nose is not accurate, and requires a great deal of rework. Clear plastic parts are provided for the camera windows, and these could be used after the nose is reworked. For the serious modeler we suggest the modification of a Hasegawa F-4E to an RF-4C. We simply cannot recommend the IMC kit even if you can find one.

<u>Testors 1/48th Scale RF-4C</u>

After looking at some of the excellent kits that Testors has recently released, we looked forward to this kit with high hopes. Our anticipation was heightened by the fact that no other kit of the RF-4 existed in this scale. However, after looking at the kit we were disappointed.

The outline and shape of this kit are accurate, and that means an excellent model can be built If the modeler adds the details that Testors left off. It is in the area of detailing where we were disappointed.

The cockpit fits into the fuselage leaving gaps between the consoles and fuselage sides. There are details molded into the fuselage sides, but these are not accurate, and lose their significance when you look at those gaps next to them. There are also gaps

ESCI/Scalecraft F-4C/D in 1/48th scale. Decals are from Bare Metal Sheet No. 4.

Testors RF-4C in 1/48th scale. ECM pods are from Monogram F-4 and F-15 kits.

behind both seats where you can look down to the bottom of the fuselage. There is a gap in front of the rear instrument panel that must be filled. More large holes exist between the consoles and the instrument panels where the auxillary panels should be. We used seventeen pieces of scrap plastic in the cockpit of our model to make it look right.

The seats are marginal, fitting together vertically down the middle leaving a sizeable gap. At the top, there is some framework on which the piece with the face curtain rings is to be mounted. We have never seen this framework on any seat in any Phantom we have ever examined or photographed.

Two instrument panels are provided for the front cockpit, but the instruction sheet tells you to throw the wrong one away. The RF-4C has two scopes at the top of the front instrument panel mounted side by side. Yet Testors would have you use the instrument panel that comes to a point at the top rather than the one that provides room for these scopes. Take a look at the photos of the front instrument panel in this book, and you will see what we mean.

Three fuel tanks are provided, two 370 gallon tanks, and one 600 gallon tank for the centerline station, and that is the extent of the external stores. There are no locator pins on these tanks, so be sure to get the 370 gallon tanks lined up correctly,, and have them nose-to-nose. Oherwise the rib on the outside of the tanks will be in the wrong position.

Both types of inboard pylons are provided, but the ones with the curved leading edge are far too thin from top to bottom. We suggest using the pylons with the straight leading edge since they are still most prevalent on the RF-4C. If the aircraft you are modeling has the curved pylons, we suggest you use the pylons from a Monogram kit. The addition of ECM pods from other kits will also add a lot to the appearance of the model.

Surface detailing is sparse. For example, the bleed air vents, molded into the Monogram and ESCI kits, are decals in this kit. The grills at the rear of the fairings that replace the forward Sparrow missile bays are missing. The pylons lack the anti-sway braces, and the surface scribing is of the raised variety and is rather crude.

All of this may sound like we are really "down" on this kit, but it does have some good points. Landing gear and wheel wells are nicely done, and the main gear has the wider tires and appropriate bulges for the Air Force version. The flare ejector on the left side of the empennage can be shown in the open position, and the tail hook can be shown in the lowered position. Fit is generally good except for where the wing meets fuselage. Here a bit of filling and sanding will be required.

It should be noted that only the older nose with the straight underside is provided. Be careful to insure that the aircaft you are modeling has this nose rather than the curved one.

Decals are provided by Scalemaster, and are excellent. Markings are for an RF-4C of the 363rd TRW, and an RF-4B of Marine VMFP-3. The only catch is that you cannot build an RF-4B from this kit since it has the wing bulges and larger tires.

This kit can be made into an excellent model, but it will take some work to bring it up to the detailed standards of the Monogram and ESCI kits. But since the required work is within the capabilities of most modelers, we recommend this kit.

CONVERSION NOSES

Both Airmodel and AIRTEC have released conversion noses for the RF-4C. Both represent the nose with the flat underside. Neither one is an accurate representation of the RF-4 nose, and most modelers could do a better job converting the nose from scratch.

DECAL SUMMARY

Note: It is impossible to completely review decals unless the reviewer has actually used the decals on a model to see how they fit. Additionally, markings on a given aircraft can be changed from time to time, so it is possible that the decals may be accurate for one point in time and not another. Therefore, this section is more of a listing of decals available than a review. Review comments are made only in regard to fit when we have actually used the decals or as to accuracy when the evidence clearly indicated an error.

Only F-4C, F-4D, and RF-4C markings are covered.

1/72nd SCALE

<u>Aerodecal No. 25A</u>

This unique sheet provides the basis for building a representative F-4 from every operational unit within

USAFE at one point in time. The markings include the unit insignia, tail codes, and tail numbers for ten different F-4C, D, E, and RF-4C aircraft. The F-4C, D, and RF-4C markings are as follows:

F-4C; AF 63-7467, 52nd TFW, 81st TFS, Spangdahlem AB, Germany (F-4C-16-MC)

F-4D; AF 66-720, 36th TFW, 53rd TFS, Bitburg AB, Germany (F-4D-29-MC)
AF 65-703, 50th TFW, 10th TFS, Hahn AB, Germany (F-4D-28-MC)
AF 66-765, 48th TFW, Lakenheath, UK (F-4D-28-MC)
AF 64-232, 81st TFW, 92nd TFS, Woodbridge AB, UK (appears to be a bogus serial number and probably is AF 66-232 as an F-4D-29-MC)

RF-4C; AF 69-374, 26th TRW, 38th TRS, Zweibruken, Germany (RF-4C-43-MC)
AF 64-1019, 10th TRW, 30th TRS, Alconbury AB, UK (RF-4C-21-MC)

ESCI No. 88

This sheet contains markings for six F-4B/C/D/E/K aircraft. The markings are printed on a heavy yellow film. The following markings are available on the sheet:

F-4C; AF 63-7633, 347th TFW, 35th TFS, Yakota AB, Japan (F-4C-21-MC)

F-4D; AF 67-14873, 306th FS, Imperial Iranian Air Force (F-4D-35-MC)

Microscale

72-164 This sheet contains instrument panels, walkways, formation lights, arresting hook placards, static port markings, rescue placards, and numerous data stencils. Black and red stencils are included.

72-237 This sheet is identical to sheet 72-164 except that the black stenciling has been replaced with white stenciling. However USAF F-4's that use white stenciling still use black stenciling on the tan areas and light gray undersurfaces. Therefore a combination of 72-164 and 72-237 is required.

72-76 Markings are provided for four F-4C's and two F-4E's on this sheet. The F-4C's are as follows:

F-4C; AF 64-665, 12th TFW, 557th TFS, named "Hell's Angel" with a coiled rattlesnake. (F-4C-21-MC)
AF 63-7413, 12th TFW, 559th TFS, named "Blue Avenger." (F-4C-15-MC)
AF 63-7522 12th TFW, 556th TFS, named "Saintly Sinner." (F-4C-20-MC)
AF 63-7604, 12 TFW, 559th TFS, named "Sugar Foot III." (F-4C-20-MC)

72-112 This sheet provides markings for two F-4C's, one RF-4C and three F-4E's. The F-4C's and RF-4C are as follows:

F-4C; AF 64-807, 432nd TRS, Udorn RTAB, Thailand. Named "Hillbilly Slick." (F-4C-24-MC)
AF-64-829, 8th TFW, 555th TFS, Ubon RTAB, Thailand. Flown by Col. Robin Olds. Nicknamed "SCAT." Two MiG kills on splitter plate (F-4C-34-MC)

RF-4C; AF 64-1033, 432nd TRW, 11th TRS, Udorn RTAB, Thailand. Named "Ol Bullet." (RF-4C-21-MC)

72-144 This is a MiG Killer sheet with markings for an F-86E, an F-105D, Col. Tomb's MiG-21, and two F-4D's.

F-4D; AF 66-7463, 555 TFS, Udorn RTAB, flown by Steve Ritchie for his first and fifth kills. (F-4D-29-MC)
AF 66-7554, 555th TFS, Udorn RTAB. Named "Trapper," this aircraft has a figure of Snoopy on the left air intake (F-4D-30-MC)

72-198 This sheet provides markings for eight F-4E's, two F-4C's and two F-4D's. The F-4C's and F-4D's are as follows:

F-4C; AF-64-937, North Dakota ANG. "The Happy Hooligans." This aircraft is listed on the sheet as an F-4D, but the serial number indicates an F-4C-24-MC.

F-4C; AF 63-460, 57th FIS, ADC. This aircraft has the 1976 William Tell "Arrow and Apple" on the fuel tanks, so we asked a friend who was a pilot in the 57th FIS in 1976 to comment on these decals, and the 48th scale decals for the same aircraft on Microscale sheet 48-72. Here are his comments:

First of all, the 57th FIS did not operate F-4Ds as the instruction sheet claims this aircraft is. The serial number indicates this aircraft is an F-4C-17-MC. The apple and arrow are the wrong colors and the arrow should be centered on the apple. The knight on the bear marking on the tanks was never used while he was in the unit in 1976. There was a map of Iceland in black with "57 FIS" on it in white in the location where Microscale shows the bear and knight design. The checkerboard design on the left side of the tail is backward. The checks on the horizontal tails are the wrong size and positioned incorrectly. There is a checkerboard design for the front nose gear door on the decal sheet, but the instruction sheet does not show where it is located. (On the 48th scale sheet, the decal is not even provided.) The aircraft should have the rounded pylons for the inboard pylons, not the straight ones as shown on the sheet. In short, these decals are unusable. See photo of this aircraft on page 12.

F-4D; AF 66-7649, 49th TFW, Holloman AFB, commander's aircraft. F-4D-30-MC. Names on canopy rails have been omitted.
AF 66-8793, 52nd TFW, 23rd TFS. (F-4D-33-MC)

72-224 This sheet includes markings for two F-4E's and two F-4C's.

F-4C; AF 63-7584, 58th TFW, commander's aircraft from Luke AFB. This aircraft has a stylized tail number with the "58" enlarged emphasizing the 58th TFW. It also has large black and white visibility stripes. (F-4C-19-MC)
AF 63-7676, 58th TFW, bicentennial aircraft. This aircraft has a colorful red, white, and blue tail fin with the "76, 76" in the tail number emphasized. (F-4C-21-MC)

Modeldecal No. 2

The well illustrated instruction sheet shows complete markings for an F-4B, Fleet Air Arm FG.1, and an F-4C.

F-4C; AF 63-7663, 8th TFW, 555 TFS, Ubon RTAB, Thailand. Flown by Col. Robin Olds. This aircraft makes an interesting companion to his SCAT MiG killer found on Microscale sheet 72-112. (F-4C-21-MC)

1/48th SCALE

Aerodecal No. 27C

Same as Aerodecal sheet No. 25A except that this sheet is in 1/48th scale.

Bare Metal No. 4

This sheet provides very colorful markings for three F-4C's of the Michigan ANG.

F-4C; AF 63-7534, all gray aircraft named "Defiance II." (F-4C-19-MC)
AF 63-7529, all gray aircraft, no name. (F-4C-19-MC)
AF 63-7626, camouflaged aircraft, (F-4C-20-MC)

Fowler (No number)

This sheet has markings for two F-4C's.

F-4C; AF 63-7664, in early light gull gray over white. Some "backdating" of the aircraft will have to be done for this F-4 (F-4C-21-MC)
AF 63-7589 of the Michigan ANG. The "Michigan" on the tail markings in the wrong style and is too small. (F-4C-19-MC)

48-67   This is a sheet that contains data and stenciling for the F-4. Data is in black, red, and yellow. The biggest problem with this sheet is the instruction sheet. The diagrams showing the location of the markings is too small and, in many cases, illegible even with a magnifying glass. This is particularly true for the access doors.

48-76   Same as sheet 48-67 above, except black markings are changed to white. Must be used with 48-67 for Air Force F-4's having standard camouflage schemes since white stenciling is used only over the green areas if it is used at all. Black is used over tan and light gray.

48-34   This sheet provides markings for a USMC F-4J and a USAF F-4C.

    F-4C; AF 63-7584, 58th TFW, commander's aircraft. Luke AFB. (Same as on sheet 72-224)

48-72   This sheet claims to provide markings for two F-4D's and a Navy F-4. In fact there is one F-4C and one F-4D. The markings for the F-4C have numerous errors.

    F-4C; AF 63-7460, 57th FIS, ADC. This is not an F-4D as claimed, but an F-4C-17-MC. See notes for this aircraft on sheet 72-198.

    F-4D; AF 66-8793, 52nd TFW, 23rd TFS, Spangdahalem AB, Germany. (F-4D-33-MC)

48-46   This sheet contains markings for two Navy F-4B's and an F-4C.

    F-4C; AF 64-937, North Dakota ANG. Same as on sheet 76-198. (F-4C-24-MC)

Detail & Scale Decals

0148   This is the first sheet released by Detail & Scale, and it contains markings for three F-4C's.

    F-4C; AF 63-7618, 57th FIS, ADC, flown by Captain (then Lt.) Lee Gerstacker. Has bicentennial and William Tell markings. (F-4C-20-MC)
    AF 63-7576, Air Defense Weapons Center, commander's aircraft in all gray scheme. (F-4C-19-MC)
    AF 64-0785, Hawaii ANG all gray scheme. (F-4C-23-MC)

0248   This sheet contains markings for three wing commander's F-4D's.

    F-4D; AF 65-731, 31st TFW, Homestead AFB, Florida. Command stripes on tail and fuselage. (F-4D-28-MC)

    F-4D; AF 64-949, 49th TFW, Holloman AFB, New Mexico. Command stripes on tail.

    F-4D; AF 65-756, 56th TFW, McDill AFB, Florida. Command stripes on tail.

1/32nd SCALE

Aerodecal No. 26B

Same as Aerodecal sheet No. 25A except that this sheet is in 1/32nd scale.

Microscale

32-30   Contains markings for two F-4E's and one F-4C.

    F-4C; AF 63-7470, 18th TFW, 67th TFS, Kadena AB, Okinawa. Named "Rub-A-Dub-Dub, two men in a tub." Instructions claim this to be an F-4D, but in fact it is an F-4C-18-MC.

REFERENCE LISTING

Note: Listed here are references on the Phantom that should prove helpful in providing information and photographs of a different nature and format than what is presented in this publication. With each listing is a brief description of what that reference covers. There are many fine references on the F-4 Phantom and they all cannot be listed here. The fact that a given reference is not included in this list is not intended to reflect unfavorably on that reference.

1. Gunston, W.T., F-4 Phantom, Charles Scribner's Sons, New York, 1977.

Excellent coverage of the developmental and operational history of the Phantom includes all versions and user nations. Most complete historical reference.

2. O'Rourke, G.G. The F-4 Phantom II, Aero Publishers, Fallbrook, California, 1979 (Previously published by Arco Publishing Co., Inc., New York, 1969.).

General historical coverage of the Phantom II up to 1969. Written by a former commanding officer of a Navy F-4 squadron. Lots of photographs of early Phantoms, but none are in color.

3. Drendel, Lou, Phantom II, A Pictorical History of the McDonnell Douglas F-4 Phantom II, Squadron/Signal Publications, Carrollton, Texas, 1977.

As the title indicates, this book has minimal text, but is filled with a great number of photos and paintings of the F-4. Covers some details, and all versions of the Phantom are illustrated.

4. Drendel, Lou, F-4 Phantom II in Action, Squadron/Signal Publications, Carrollton, Texas, 1972.

Many good black and white photographs of the Phantom "in action." Contains accounts of missions flown in SEA by both Navy and Air Force pilots.

5. Drendel, Lou, . . . And Kill MiGs, Squadron/Signal Publications, Carrollton, Texas, 1974.

While not exclusively devoted to the Phantom, this book covers the MiG killing missions flown by the F-4 and its pilots. Illustrations include photos and drawings of some of the Phatoms that shot down MiGs over Vietnam.

6. Ward, Richard and Rene J. Francillon, McDonnell F-4 Phantom II in U.S. Navy, USMC, USAF, RAF, FAA, RAFF, Luftwaffe and Foreign Service, Osprey Publishing Limited, England, 1972. (Volume 1)

Basically a picture book, this publication covers markings carried by many Phantoms. Illustrated with photos, drawings and paintings.

7. Ward, Richard and Rene J. Francillon, McDonnell F-4 Phantom II in USAF, U.S. Navy, USMC, RAF, FAA, Luftwaffe, and IIAF Service, Osprey Publishing Limited, England, 1973 (Volume 2).

Volume II of number 6 above.

8. F-4C, D, M, Phantom II, Koku Fan Special Number 57, Burindo Publications, Burin-do, Japan, 1975.

Excellent photographic coverage of the F-4C, D, and M with emphasis on markings. Japanese text.

9. F-4C/D Phantom II, Koku Fan Special Number 124, Burindo Publications, Burin-do, Japan, 1981.

Typical Koku Fan coverage with emphasis on markings. More detailed coverage than usual. Japanese text.

10. "RF-4 Photo Phantoms," Aerophile, Volume 2, Number 4, Page 2.

Although we intended to limit this listing to books, this article, that came out just as we went to press, is so complete and excellent in its coverage of reconnaissance Phantoms that we have included it here. It contains more information on these versions than any book we have seen.